hip hop beats, indigenous rhymes

SUNY SERIES, NATIVE TRACES

Jace Weaver and Scott Richard Lyons, editors

hip hop beats, indigenous rhymes

MODERNITY AND HIP HOP IN INDIGENOUS NORTH AMERICA

kyle t. mays

SUNY
PRESS

Published by State University of New York Press, Albany

For information, contact State University of New York Press,
Albany, NY
www.sunypress.edu

Library of Congress Cataloging-in-Publication Data

Names: Mays, Kyle, author.
Title: Hip hop beats, indigenous rhymes : modernity and hip hop in
    indigenous North America / Kyle T. Mays.
Description: Albany : State University of New York Press, 2018. | Series:
    Native traces | Includes bibliographical references and index.
Identifiers: LCCN 2017024529 (print) | LCCN 2017031345 (ebook) |
    ISBN 9781438469478 (e-book) | ISBN 9781438469454 (hardcover :
    alk. paper) | ISBN 9781438469461 (pbk. : alk. paper)
Subjects: LCSH: Indians of North America--Music--History and
    criticism. | Rap (Music)—History and criticism. | Hip-hop—North
    America.
Classification: LCC ML3531 (ebook) | LCC ML3531 .M29 2018 (print) |
    DDC 782.421649089/97—dc23
LC record available at https://lccn.loc.gov/2017024529

10 9 8 7 6 5 4 3 2 1

TO RJ, DJ, JASMINE, HAYDEN, ANGELA,
BRANDON, JJ, CHERISH, AND MAKIAH;
KEEP WORKING HARD.

AND TO **ALL MY BAD AND BOUGIE
INDIGENOUS MILLENNIALS**, WITH LOVE.

CONTENTS

A NOTE ON LANGUAGE
Black English and Uncensored Mode

Black Language

Whenever I open up a book on hip hop culture, or any ethnic/racial group, I first ask if that writer honors, respects, and utilizes the language of the particular group that he or she is writing about. I ask this not because I believe in racial essentialism, but because I believe that different ways of being and cultural expression, through language, should be valued in a variety of contexts, whether in the church or on the block. Given all of the work that scholars have done in language and literacy, education, and the advocacy of various linguistic practices, I assume and hope that people will also do that when writing about hip hop culture, which is also related to black ways of speaking and knowing.

Black language is legitimate. By black language, I mean African American vernacular English, Black English, US Ebonics, and a host of other names. (Please note that there are other varieties and these can vary regionally and even geographically; there is, for example, black language in the Caribbean.) From Mark Twain's *Huckleberry Finn* to Lorenzo Dowd Turner in the early twentieth century to the work of the queen of black language, Geneva Smitherman, aka Dr. G, in the late twentieth and early part of the twenty-first centuries, the use and study of black language and culture has existed and continues to thrive as a subject of academic inquiry.

According to Smitherman, Black English is "Euro-American speech with an Afro-American meaning, nuance, tone, and gesture."[1] Smitherman further argues that Black English has two parts: language and style. That is, while there is the technical, linguistic part of the language, there is also the style in which that language is employed—better yet, the philosophy embedded in that language.[2] The word "language" is crucial here.

The distinction between a dialect and a language as it relates to Black English is also crucial. "A language can easily be seen to be legitimately different from another language, whereas dialects are often viewed as mere corruptions of or departures from a given language."[3] The issue is more political than linguistic, and is based upon the belief in the superiority of so-called standard American English. My aim is not to defend the legitimacy of Black English as a language because, frankly, I do consider it a language based upon the existing data. However, it is important for those studying hip hop in other non-black contexts (even those outside of the United States) to consider how non-black diasporic subjects who appropriate hip hop, also appropriate blackness, especially linguistically, and how this dual appropriation enters into their rapping.

I deploy and employ it throughout this book as naturally as I can. There are several reasons for this. For one, we can have hip hop studies and hundreds of books and articles on the topic, while people be quotin' its lyrics and commentin' on its aesthetics; yet, don't nobody be usin' it in their own writing. In essence, they acknowledge and respect the culture, but only in a non-academic setting, and certainly not in written form. I find this amazing, if not problematic. There are, of course, exceptions—you can check the notes for that—but we can't continue to cater to the standards of "whitestream" academia in the twenty-first century. (With that said, big shout out to SUNY Press for lettin' me freestyle a bit. Much love.)

Second, to not use black language reinforces the idea that one form of language is more legitimate than the other; in this case, so-called standard English, what Smitherman calls the "Language of Wider" (or "Whiter"; she know she be signifyin'!) communication. I refuse to engage in the politics of linguistic subjugation by ignoring black language. Though black and Indigenous, I was raised by a single mother from the projects of Cleveland who taught me the beauty of language; it was not until I went to school that I began to experience linguistic discrimination. It is time I reclaim my humanity.

As hip hop culture, especially language, has gone global, corporations done started using black language in their advertisements. McDonalds be using "I'm lovin' it," droppin' the G. Black language exists in everyday forms of communication, especially with texting.

For example, one of my homies texted me recently sayin', "you cray." Many people use this, but what does it actually represent? It is a form of copula deletion. I don't wanna get all linguistically heavy, so lemme explain: In LWC, they would say, "you are cray," because that is the proper way to say it. In black language, you drop the subject; in the LWC, you keep it. Yet, both suggest the same thing. So, where did this language come from? Hip hop. People have the nerve to call black folks ignorant when they don't even know that black language is a legitimate thing, at least according to linguists who are trained in such a thing.

Finally, as I mentioned, hip hop is everywhere. I can go into a club full of European Americans who know the lyrics verbatim, even better than I do. They mansplain to me. Mansplaining refers to how men feel the need, based upon their privilege, to explain something to women and those with less privilege in society because they *know* better. I can't count the number of times I have been chillin' in a hipster bar and some zaughanush will begin to hip-hopsplain, telling *me* about the golden age of hip hop or some obscure-ass underground artist who reminds them of Tupac, who will breathe life back into hip hop. I repeat: Hip hop is everywhere. So, too, is black language.[4] Therefore, uhma be usin' it throughout this book.

Uncensored Speech

Shit, I'm pretty sure my grandma, a sanctified woman of God, would not be happy with this section, or this book. Nevertheless, it needs to be said. Throughout this book, I curse, swear, and use so-called obscene, uncouth language. There is a linguistic madness to my deployment and employment. In his brilliant essay "African American Language Use: Ideology and So-Called Obscenity" (1998), linguist Arthur Spears suggests that we should think carefully about how we judge language, and what standards we apply to the use of language,

> [R]ather, it reflects one of the major conclusions presented below . . . rigorous analysis of form, meaning, and communicative behavior is required before one can pass judgment on the speech of members

of communities other than one's own, where the term community membership is determined by age, socioeconomic class, ethnicity, gender, and other variables.[5]

Spears is referring to what he calls "uncensored mode." He describes this mode of speaking as: "expressions that in censored contexts are considered obscene or [of an] evaluatively neutral way."[6] Importantly, uncensored mode exists in languages around the world, but what he is referring to is the normalization of obscene language and what it might mean. In uncensored mode, the "obscene" language is "not inherently negative or positive." Rather, words can be "negative, positive, or neutral in force depending on how they are used."[7] What this basically means is that we assign value to certain ways of speaking over others. Language depends on the context, including audience. Cursing, just like any form of language, is not necessarily positive or negative, if understood as such. In other words, while one may not swear at Catholic Mass, later that day, after a few drinks at the crib, you might start cussin' like a sailor!

Thus, I use so-called obscene language throughout the book. For the most part, my intent is positive or neutral. Though I'm sure if you get offended or don't like an argument or my interpretation, the swearing gon' feel quite negative; I'm okay with that. I would, however, recommend that before you get all frustrated about my use of language, check your privilege, by asking yourself these questions: 1) am I mad because I disagree with there being such a thing as black language because I have read the studies and I'm qualified to talk about it?, 2) do I believe there is only one way to write an academic book?, and 3) am I mad about something else, and *maybe* it's a bit deeper than language? To quote Eduardo Bonilla-Silva, you might be participating in what he calls "racism without racists." To quote Dr. G, let's stop the "mis-education of the negro—and you too." Bless yo' heart. I know you ain' racist, but I want to help you think beyond linguistic norms.

ACKNOWLEDGMENTS

Yo, straight up, writing a book is hard as hell. For me, it's not the writing per se; I like to write. However, when you're carrying other people's stories, sharing their art and words, there is another level of responsibility because you want to make sure you're expressing yourself and them, honestly. To all the Indigenous hip hop artists whose work I relied on and used, much love and respect. Miigwetch for creating art that the world needs, that Indigenous youth need. You're a part of the Indigenous Millennials who are keeping our cultures alive and strong. We have not disappeared, and with your art, you're letting these settlers know that we ain' going nowhere. Much love.

I also want to thank my mother. She's a bad mom (bad meaning good). She took care of five children for the most part by herself. I've seen her struggle, but she never lost her integrity as a parent and still loves us to this day. Now, Mom, please tell the world that I'm your favorite child so your other children know! This brings me to my next thank yous.

Big shout to my siblings: Shaun, Yaya, Twin, and Jay. I love you all. You're the best siblings anyone can have. My sisters always have my back, literally down to throw them hands for their brother. Yaya is always a bundle of roasts and haterade, who I wouldn't trade for anyone. I love my Twin; I wouldn't trade sharing a womb with anyone else (I did come out first, so quit actin' like the big sis when you the lil' sis, LOL). My older brother is a bad dude, been practicing martial arts, including Jeet Kune Do, since he was young. He would never let anyone mess with his li'l bro. He also had to serve as a father figure and older brother to me all at the same time he was growing up. #Respect. (Oh, I been practicing, bro, so the next time I see you watch out!). Finally, I gotta thank my little brother Jay. He's the kindest and most outgoing of all of us, and loves to sing. He will go from gospel to Justin Bieber to the latest rap song in one setting. He has a tender heart, which I have learned a great deal from.

I'd also like to thank my fam: Dr. Geneva Smitherman "Dr. G," AJ Rice, Dr. David Kirkland, Dr./Reverend Jeff Robinson, Dr. Austin Jackson, and Dr. Ashley Newby. They've always pushed me to be about my business and to work hard, since I was at Michigan State University. They've seen me grow and continue to support me. I hope I meet your lofty expectations. We need to get together at the fish market soon!

I would also like to thank my homies Dr. Kevin Whalen, Eduardo "E" Coronel, and Dr. Bryce Henson. You all have supported me with laughs, roasts, brown ale, and Jameson. Thanks for being there, and I hope to see you soon.

I wouldn't be where I am without my social media fam. I have to give a big shout to my homies who always talk shit with me on Twitter: again, Bryce Henson, Dr. Dallas Hunt, and (soon to be Dr.) Susan Blight. They make me laugh and think every day. Chi miigwetch and much love. Now, when are you all gonna come kick it with me in LA?

I need to give a big shout out to my acquisitions editor, Amanda Lanne-Camilli. She believed in this project from the beginning and has been very supportive. I'm really excited to be in Jace Weaver and Scott Richard Lyons' series. They found really fantastic anonymous readers; so big shout to you all!

I think it is important to acknowledge those who support you and those who motivate you in other ways. For instance, big shout to the haters. You give me all the motivation I need. Miigwetch, and smile.

Finally, I would like to thank my fellow Indigenous Millennials. I hope I represented you well, and I'm proud to be living in this moment. Let's keep on resisting and building, for if we can take anything from our ancestors, it is this: We gon' be alright—just like they were!

CAN WE LIVE AND BE MODERN AND INDIGENOUS?

Toward an Indigenous Hip Hop Culture

In the summer of 2009, I attended an academic conference on the West Coast. It was arid and hot. Held during the evening, we had a fancy gathering with fresh-grilled steak, fish, and all sorts of fancy foods that at the time I was not culturally equipped to know what they were. Not knowing very many people, I got my plate, then scoped out where I was going to sit. I approached a table with what looked like a healthy mix of elders and adults in their early thirties, then sat down. An elder took an interest in me. He was a very tall, handsome, masculine Native (Dine) man. He had long gray hair that glistened in the setting sun; he wore a bolo tie. His hands were adorned with at least three rings on each. And he had a deep voice; he sounded like my uncle.

He asked me where I was from (basically, are you Native and if so, where is your family from? I found this a positive approach to the question.). And finally, he asked me what I was interested in academically. I told him that I was interested in the relationship between black Americans and Native Americans during the black-red-power movements. He nodded, searching, I suppose, about how he could follow up with another question or extend the discussion. Sensing the pause, I then casually mentioned that I am interested in Native American hip hop. His head jerked up as if he had a sudden neck spasm. His eyes, now fixed on me, were draped with the wrinkles of knowledge and wisdom.

The elder paused. He rubbed his chin, slightly rocking, seeking a way to respond to my comment. Excited, I leaned in. Finally coming to a response, he said, "You know, there's a lot of gang activity on the reservation." Shocked, I paused, waiting for more commentary. He said

1

nothing further about hip hop. We talked about something else, some-thing that I have suppressed.

My mind was racing. How did we go from talking about hip hop to the problem of gang activity on the reservation? Gang activity and hip hop, at least for me, is a non sequitur. I just could not get over that.

Having reflected on that moment over the last several years, I have come to this conclusion: the elder, bless his heart, equated hip hop, or blackness, with increased gang activity on the reservation. (I never did get a chance to ask for evidence of this; I guess I just chose not to disrespect my elders.) The "urban" is supposedly where premodern Native people go, lose their "traditions," and bring back the negative aspects of cities to the rez, which impacts social relations. Unfortunately, this urban-rez dichotomy continues in scholarship.[1] Indeed, Hilary Weaver, a scholar in social work, writes, "An urban context can have a negative influence on Native American youth. Deviant peer norms and a 'city lifestyle' can promote high risk behaviors and can be incompatible with the cultural immersion found on reservations."[2]

There are several problems with this statement. First, Weaver assumes that Native people and cities are incompatible. In going through the author's footnotes, she cites scholarship that argues that Native people are essentially immigrants to cities, mostly prompted by termination and relocation policies in the postwar era.[3] These policies included the Relocation Act of 1956, and were designed to end the so-called Native dependency on the US government for resources, even though it was their treaty obligation. Couched in the language of assimilating into the American dream, Native nations quickly realized that these policies were designed to assimilate Native people into the American way of life, or, to put it more bluntly, make them white and erase their Indigenous heritage. Today, some Native and non-Native folks have come to view urban Native people as not being "real" Indigenous people because they grew up primarily in urban cultural and spatial contexts.

Weaver's perspective suggests that Native people are recent migrants to cities, similar to white ethnics of earlier periods. Yet, recent historical scholarship has begun to challenge such a deficit perspective, offering counter narratives that put Native people squarely in the realm of modernity and city development.[4]

Second, the author's comments suggest that the urban code for black and Latinx produces negative consequences for Native people, who are supposed to be pristine, innocent, stoic people who do not live in the modern world. In case the author did not know, most Native people live in cities throughout Canada and the United States.[5] The author perpetuates the idea that the urban environment is bad because it is poor and inhabited by black and brown folks; history reveals to us that many urban places were deliberately constructed this way.[6] I am not suggesting that cities are a bastion for peace and prosperity. However, not all is bad in cities, and much cultural exchange takes place within those spaces. Many Native people thrive in cities, and it allows them to expand their cultural repertoire. One of the most important things about the urban culture that has influenced Indigenous people has been hip hop culture.

In this book, I make one major claim: Indigenous hip hop might be one of the most important cultural forces that has hit Indigenous North America since the Ghost Dance movement in the late nineteenth century.[7] Straight up! Hip hop allows for Indigenous people, through culture, to express themselves as modern subjects. They can use it to move beyond the persistent narratives of their demise, or their invisibility, or the notion that they are people of the past incapable of engaging with modernity.

Now, let the story begin.

Hip Hop Beats, Indigenous Rhymes analyzes how Native hip hop artists challenge colonialism/racism, and at times, how they are complicit in perpetuating settler ideas of what it means to be Indigenous, construct identity, and present themselves as modern subjects. Placing Indigenous hip hop within the ongoing struggle of oppressed people in North America, especially black Americans who have used hip hop to challenge their own subjugation, this book argues that Indigenous hip hop is the latest and newest assertion of Indigenous sovereignty throughout Indigenous North America. Indigenous hip hop is here to stay, and it is something that we need to discuss and respect.

Based upon interviews with Native hip hop artists, analyses of music and videos, and other media sources, this book argues that hip hop is not only an assertion of Indigenous sovereignty, but also a postmodern Indigenous popular culture that is not bound by mainstream and conservative ideas about what it means to be Indigenous. Instead, it illustrates how Native hip hop artists are constructing a variety of identities that serve as a model for how Native communities might reject the "colonial politics of recognition."[8] Before continuing, I want to define Indigenous hip hop.

Writers of hip hop have consistently argued that hip hop culture consists of four elements: graffiti, break dancing (b-boy and b-girl), emceeing, and deejaying. Within the last fifteen years, hip hop studies scholars have expanded the elements to include various forms of media like Internet and other forms of expression such as magazines and blogs. Activism has been a major part of hip hop from the beginning, either in the form of protest music or community activism.

Indigenous hip hop includes all of the above, but is uniquely engaged with Native cultures and realities. I define Indigenous hip hop as the culture adopted and produced by Native people who are using this culture to challenge settler colonialism, white supremacy, and heteropatriarchy, among other things. I want to reiterate that one of the failures of much of the scholarship in hip hop studies is a focus on the "positive" things that hip hop artists do. Admittedly, I do that in some ways, too. There are artists who are not much interested in challenging heteropatriarchy or imagining alternative forms of gender identities; they ain' even trying. However, there are those working to create an alternative future for Native people, through hip hop, and my goal is to highlight some of the happenings in Indigenous hip hop at this moment. The two major goals of Indigenous hip hop artists are obtaining Native sovereignty and asserting themselves as modern Native people, which is a key and unique feature of Indigenous hip hop. Other groups use hip hop to assert their humanity; Indigenous people have to convince others that they exist.

While other groups do have to deal with stereotypes, in a settler society that is predicated on Indigenous dispossession, white men have systematically created the idea for society at large that Native people have disappeared, which is something that other groups do not have to deal with. Given this context, having to assert a Native identity through hip hop is a remarkable task, and while it is difficult to quantify whether or not Native people have been successful in this endeavor (as far as reaching a mainstream white and black American audience), they do have a good social media following, which is important to their brand.

Hip Hop Studies: A State of the Field and Why It Needs Indigeneity

Over the last thirty years, hip hop studies scholarship has exploded. While there was hip hop scholarship in the 1980s, the field of hip hop studies really began with the work of Tricia Rose, whose *Black Noise: Rap Music and Black Culture in Contemporary America* (1994) introduced a new method for studying hip hop. Using black cultural theories, Rose analyzed lyrics, videos, interviews, and followed the media coverage of hip hop in a variety of presses. These methodological approaches helped her to understand and explain a movement that had taken the world by storm. Ever the intellectual prophetess, it was Rose's desire that hip hop would "foster the development of more globally focused projects."[9] Her words proved prophetic. Since then, the scholarship has gone global. Scholars such as Ian Condry have identified the intersection of blackness and Japanese identity through hip hop culture and other places around the globe.[10] Others such as H. Samy Alim have worked to understand youth culture, hip hop, and language's role in it.[11] Hip hop's global turn inspired hip hop journalist Jeff Chang to proclaim, "It's a Hip Hop world."[12]

Hip hop studies is now a serious academic field of critical inquiry. Hip hop has become a part of the elite institutions of the world. There is even a Hip Hop Archive at Harvard University. Hip hop journalist Jeff Chang teaches at Stanford University. Rice University even invited rapper Bun B to teach a course.[13] Hip hop has and will continue to be an academic pursuit. However, even with all of these great changes and hip hop's global reach, there is little scholarship on Indigenous hip hop.[14] Very few scholars have even broached the topic of indigeneity in hip hop culture. Those who have analyzed indigeneity have mostly written on hip hop culture in Australia and New Zealand. Many studies in North America have remained in the vaults of libraries as dissertations and theses.[15] Consequently, there is a need for a book that critically explores not only indigeneity within hip hop culture, but also how Indigenous people construct themselves as Indigenous *and* modern subjects, and how they contribute to the sovereignty through hip hop of Indigenous communities.

Hip hop scholars have a major role to play in continuing to develop the field and bridging both the cultural producers and the intellectuals. As hip hop studies and youth culture scholar S. Craig Watkins writes, "In its effort to realize its unique role in the struggle for hip hop, the intelligentsia must help pose the tough questions and offer the critical, though not always favorable, insight that captures the passion, predilections, and perils that define the movement."[16] It is in this light that I see my role, and I hope other scholars of Indigenous hip hop also begin doing the same thing: documenting the good, the bad, and the not-so-pretty aspects of Indigenous hip hop. We have a responsibility to document and explain Indigenous hip hop to multiple audiences, moving it from the margins of invisibility (much like what we already have to do anyway) to visibility. Above all, our role in producing scholarship on Indigenous hip hop will help further the cause of Indigenous sovereignty. If we can do nothing else, we can at least do that. And that will require that we write honestly and genuinely about what we see and hear, because sovereignty is nothing without honest conversations.

Indigenous Hip Hop: History of Black-Indigenous Cultural Exchange

The history of hip hop and its explosion into the mainstream is the quintessential version of the American dream. Blacks and Puerto Ricans founded it out of nothing. It originated in the devastated community of the South Bronx in New York City with burning buildings, decreased funding for schools, and no money. Yet with the infusion of black American, Caribbean, and Latinx cultural influences, these youths created an entire sound, dance, culture—an entire movement. Little did they know it would take the world by storm. Today, hip hop is all around the world.[17] Today, hip hop is global.

To date, there is no definitive history of Indigenous hip hop culture in North America. However, in the last few years, scholars have begun to make mention of Indigenous hip hop in their work. For instance, in his book *Heartbeat, Warble, and the Electric Powwow: American Indian Music* (2016), Craig Harris writes about Native American music; he also includes a chapter titled "Divas, Hip-Hoppers, and Electronic Dance Masters," which includes short references to Cherokee rapper Litefoot, an Ottawa-based group called a Tribe Called Red known for their "Electric Powwow sound," and Lakota rapper Frank Waln.[18] While important, the author presents only a brief snapshot into their role as hip hop artists. In addition to Harris's text, *Indigenous Pop: Native American Music from Jazz to Hip Hop* (2016), edited by Jeff Berglund, Jan Johnson, and Kimberli Lee, provides a collection of essays that illustrate the contribution of Native people's music to US musical traditions. Framing it in terms of Indigenous "pop," they challenge the very notion of "tradition." They write, "by joining 'pop' with 'Indigenous,' we are also applying pressure to some notions about traditionalism and Indigenous cultures by foregrounding that tradition is not a static category, but one that is contested and evolving."[19] While the book is far-reaching, covering Indigenous people's contributions to music, from country to jazz to rock, there are two essays on hip hop, and only one that deals explicitly with Indigenous hip hop.[20] In other parts of the Indigenous world, though, scholars have begun to document Indigenous hip hop as a single subject of intellectual inquiry.

Tony Mitchell has written at least one essay that examines the history of Aboriginal hip hop in Australia. He notes, "The history of hip hop in Australia is largely a question of often competing oral histories of local developments in various places."[21] Arguably, the same thing could be said about Indigenous hip hop. Journalist Cristina Verán has written on Indigenous hip hop since at least 2006, though namely in Australia and New Zealand. She did write a piece in *SNAG* magazine on reservation hip hop. In a 2006 interview with Jeff Chang, she stated, "I find it very exciting and encouraging that indigenous youth here and abroad—particularly those who have remained connected to their cultural identities—have actually found in hip-hop a useful tool to remain strong in their cultures."[22] Journalists have written short pieces here and there on Indigenous hip hop—and many more exist today—but we still need book-length work on the history of Indigenous hip hop, capturing its ebbs and flows in Native American country, both on the reserve/ation and in urban spaces. It is not the aim of this section to offer a definitive history of Indigenous hip hop, although someone should write that history, as it is important to acknowledge the longer history of black-Indigenous relations.

Carter G. Woodson, the "father of black history," wrote in 1920, "One of the longest unwritten chapters of the history of the United States is that treating of the relations of the Negroes and Indians."[23] In some ways, his words prove prophetic. More recently, scholars such as Tiya Miles and Sharon P. Holland have written that Afro-Indigenous histories, especially those that fit culturally in between, if you will, share some common historical themes. In a recent coauthored essay, Miles and Holland write,

> Pain and loss. Slavery and land. These terms map onto and move through one another a perhaps the primary concepts in Afro-/Native studies. Without a fertile land-base and free labor to work it, the U.S. would not have developed into the prosperous empire that it became. Land was usurped from Indigenous Americans, labor extracted from people of African as well as native descent.[24]

Black-Indigenous histories have been crossing paths with each other ever since whites began inhumanely bringing captured Africans to Turtle Island. The extent of these relationships in the cultural realm can be difficult to trace, but that should not stop us from at least speculating. As cultural theorist Paul Gilroy writes,

> the reflexive cultures and consciousness of the European settlers and those of the Africans they enslaved, the "Indians" they slaughtered, and the Asians they indentured were not, even in situations of the most extreme brutality, sealed off hermetically from each other.[25]

Written as a corrective more recently, scholar Jace Weaver argues that we should consider a "Red Atlantic" as a part of the Indigenous experience in the Western Hemisphere. Weaver argues that there are three components of the Red Atlantic, which include the flow of Native bodies and ideas, the movement of material goods, including animals and plants, and the movement of technology and literature. He asserts that the point of his own work is to contend that Native people were not marginal to the Atlantic experience, and also, I argue as I think he would, modernity; but rather, they were "as central as Africans" and Europeans in the development of the Atlantic world.[26] The same should be argued about the exchange of music.

Historian John W. Troutman has documented the Indigenous Hawaiian influence on black American music, especially when it comes to the steel guitar.[27] As Troutman indicates, cultural exchange, through music, is rarely a one-way transaction. Thus, we can and should at least speculate about the various ways in which black music influenced Indigenous music, and how Indigenous music influenced black music. My aim here, then, is to bring these processes to light, through hip hop culture.

Blackness and indigeneity intersect in Indigenous hip hop in unique ways. For the purposes of this book, I define blackness as a global, cultural phenomenon that demarcates people of African descent from other peoples. Their histories, rooted in Diaspora, especially within the Western Hemisphere are defined by trauma and movement, but also resistance and developing a sense of place. Blackness is at once global and local; it is, above all, a form of resistance to European domination. But blackness must be understood in context, within what the late historian Manning Marable called the "New Racial Domain." The NRD consists of three social, political, and economic conditions, which impact how we define the experience of black folks today: "mass unemployment, mass incarceration, and mass disenfranchisement."[28] At the beginning of the twentieth century, Du Bois defined race relations as the "problem of the color line."[29] Extending this argument, Marable suggested that the problem of the twenty-first century is "the problem of global apartheid: the racialized division and stratification of resources, wealth, and power that separates Europe, North America, and Japan from the billions of mostly black, brown, indigenous undocumented immigrant, and poor people across the planet."[30] Importantly, blackness is also an expression of culture.

Black cultural theorist Mark Anthony Neal offers a unique perspective on black culture in the postwar period. Referring to what he describes as the "post-soul aesthetic," Neal writes,

> I am surmising that there is an aesthetic center within contemporary black popular culture that at various moments considers issues like deindustrialization, desegregation, the corporate annexation of black popular expression, cybernization in the workforce, the globalization of finance and communication, the general commodification of black life and culture, and the proliferation of black "meta-identities," wile continuously collapsing on modern concepts of blackness and reanimating "premodern" (African?) concepts of blackness.[31]

Blackness, then, must be understood within all of these contexts. Blackness can be a unifying cultural, ideological, even political force. We should not forget that hip hop culture is an expression of blackness, mixed with some Latinx influences. Indigeneity is also important to hip hop, as I shall show throughout this book.

While Indigenous people are often defined by their historical relationship to a certain place and their engagement with a settler nation, I define indigeneity as a way of being Indigenous in the world, combined with other social identities, including race, class, gender, sexuality, and ability, and status and non-status. In other words, there are multiple ways of being Indigenous and belonging to an Indigenous community. The 2007 United Nations' Declaration of the Rights of the Indigenous Peoples was a major step in affirming their right to self-determination.[32] Within Indigenous studies, there is no one consensus on what indigeneity means, but I do rely on one put forth by Hawaiian scholar Maile Arvin. She writes, "in my own working definition, [indigeneity] refers to the historical and contemporary effects of colonial and anticolonial demands and desires related to a certain land or territory and the various displacements on that place's original or longtime inhabitants."[33] I would add to Arvin's definition that indigeneity also includes cultural representation, both colonial representations and Indigenous expressions of indigeneity for the purposes of cultural sovereignty.

Forms of indigeneity have always been a part of black cultural production, especially music. As Joy Harjo has stated, "go ahead/ jump holy/ all the way to the stomp grounds/we were there when Jazz was invented."[34] While she acknowledges that jazz was a black cultural product, it also has Indigenous roots. If we can say this about jazz, why can't we also say the same thing about hip hop? From its conception, drums (and beats) have been a significant part of hip hop music. Both African and Indigenous descendants continue to use the drum as a part of their musical production. Blackness and indigeneity, through sound, have intersected.

Aesthetics of indigeneity have also been a part of hip hop. Let us recall the Soul Sonic Force, led by Afrika Bambaataa. Within the group was a person named Pow Wow, who wore a headdress as well as other articles of what seem to be "indigenous"-inspired clothing. Though some might quip and simply excuse his actions, the fact is that he wore a headdress, and that is not cool, back then or today. Nevertheless, forms of indigeneity have been a part of hip hop culture. Blackness and indigeneity also intersect at the level of discourse, or language.

Language is central to how people view the world. Words are embedded with symbols and meanings.[35] Blackness, especially black language, is a part of Indigenous hip hop. As Tricia Rose explains, "Rap music is a black cultural expression that prioritizes black voices from the margins of urban America."[36] Furthermore, it is "a form of rhymed storytelling accompanied by highly rhythmic, electronically based music."[37] The key to understanding the rhythms of rap music is also to understand its origins in black culture through language. Rapping is an expression, first and foremost, of black language, only magnified.

According to critical sociolinguist Geneva Smitherman, African American language is "Euro American speech with an Afro-American tone, nuance, and gesture."[38] There are several debates about whether or not African American language is, in fact, a different language or simply a dialect.[39] Still, no one can deny its impact in the United States and around the globe, especially as hip hop has helped take it mainstream. One of the most important aspects of it is language. Smitherman also writes, "rap music is rooted in the Black oral tradition of tonal semantics, narrativizing, signification/signifyin, the dozens/playin the dozens,

Africanized syntax, and other communicative practices."[40] Language is central to how blackness is performed in hip hop culture; Native people adopt these parts of hip hop culture. Indeed, Native people rapping presents two forms of sociolinguistic construction of reality. It is what Anishinaabe literary scholar Scott Richard Lyons calls rhetorical sovereignty: "the inherent right and ability of peoples to determine their own communicative needs and desires in this pursuit to decide for themselves the goals, modes, styles, and languages of public discourse."[41] Today's rappers, as modern Indigenous orators, are engaging in two forms of language production for the purposes of Indigenous sovereignty.[42]

Black and Indigenous relations are not all good. Indeed, within a settler colonial society, Native peoples' experiences are oftentimes ignored and, even worse, rendered invisible. While blackness represents racialization, we need to also focus on how indigeneity is a result of settler colonialism. Chickasaw theorist Jodi Byrd presents an important argument for understanding these complicated intersections, "Of course, colonization relies upon racialization to facilitate, justify, and rationalize the state." But she cautions us that, "to reframe colonization as racialization at the site of radical critique risks leaving those very colonial structures intact on the one hand and allowing all experiences of oppression within settler colonialism to step forward as colonized on the other."[43] In other words, while I seek to understand these cultural intersections, I write about them cautiously, with hopes of a better future for black-Indigenous relations.

Indigenous Hip Hop and Modernity

Indigenous cultures are an important part of decolonizing ourselves in a settler colonial society. By highlighting culture, I am not excluding the material reality of the everyday needs of Indigenous communities, including land, water, food, education, housing, etc. Decolonization is a process whereby we work to cleanse ourselves of the ubiquitous nature of colonialism. That cleansing must happen daily, and it takes many forms. This means that our decolonizing efforts engage with modernity.

Although the idea of modernity is a complicated one, I mean it in its simplest form: how whites have used ideas and representations of

Indigenous people to construct their selves.[44] In this sense then, being modern is associated with being white and literally living in modern times. Being Indigenous means being nonwhite, in this case Indigenous, and lacking the ability to live in a world that has passed them by—at least that is how the narrative goes. Modernity is negatively used and mobilized not only by whites but also Indigenous people, through the rhetoric of "tradition." In contrast, I look to reclaim and regenerate the concept of Indigenous modernity to explain, in part, how hip hop helps move us toward a decolonized future, one that challenges assumptions about Indigenous people being incapable of living in the present, as modern subjects. I describe this process below.

We should embrace what Leech Lake Anishinaabe scholar Scott Richard Lyons calls "indigenous modernity." Lyons writes that, "to embrace [indigenous] modernity is to usher in other modern concepts (not all of them necessarily, but some of them, and I'd say the ones we want), including the concept of decolonization." Indigenous people have embraced hip hop as a modern culture/concept, too. Indeed, hip hop allows for Indigenous people today to create new definitions of what it means to be both Indigenous and modern. In answering to criticism that Native people engaging with hip hop is not a "traditional" practice of Indigenous people, Indigenous arts collective Beat Nation has responded accordingly,

> There has been some criticism over the years by older community members who see [Hip Hop's] influence as a break from tradition and the movement of the culture towards a pop-based mainstream assimilation. But in Beat Nation we see just the opposite happening. These artists are not turning away from the traditions as much as searching for new ways into them.[45]

Traditions are not some static things that Native people are bound by. Language is of course central to a community's survival, and big ups to those who work on language reclamation projects. However—while I appreciate ceremony and the use of language—we are people who create meanings and traditions everyday. Native people do not live in a cultural vacuum. While Native hip hop artists surely participate in what we might call "traditions," they are not bound by what that means. More than this, they create new ideas of what it means to be Indigenous.

Indigenous Hip Hop, Settler Colonialism, and Cultural Sovereignty

For Indigenous communities, the term "sovereignty" is a crucial component of everyday cultural, economic, social, and political life. In 1995, Osage theorist Robert Warrior advocated for intellectual sovereignty. He reasoned that "if our struggle is anything, it is the struggle for sovereignty, and if sovereignty is anything, it is a way of life."[46] Controlling our knowledge production and how that is represented in popular culture is very important. With the continued use of Native American imagery in settler-stream US popular culture, what Philip Deloria described as "playing Indian," we need to be very careful about how Native people and their images are represented while simultaneously challenging and producing as "accurate" Indigenous imagery as we possibly can.[47]

This is, of course, another component of intellectual sovereignty, what Michelle Raheja has called "cultural sovereignty." She has worked to make sure that we do not forget the importance of culture as a contributing force in promoting Indigenous sovereignty. "My argument about sovereignty does not stand in opposition to the works by my social science colleagues," writes Raheja.[48] Instead, "it is critical to insist on a much broader notion of sovereignty . . . in cultural forms as diverse as dance, film, theater, the plastic arts, literature, and even hip-hop and graffiti."[49] Indigenous hip hop is a part of the political, cultural, and social milieu of the Indigenous struggle for sovereignty.

Indigenous hip hop is an expression of Indigenous cultural sovereignty. It is an expression of Indigenous modernity to the max. It is also unique because of the cultural exchanges between black culture(s). It is rooted in Native history and present realities. Crucially, Indigenous hip hop is not bound by the archaic notion of Native "traditional" ways of life whatever that means. It is built on Native histories, but constructed by people who are attempting to live for the now and the future of

Indigenous sovereignty. Native hip hop artists are interested in showcasing how Native people actually live.

While hip hop is a black art form, especially in language, Indigenous people make it their own, rhyming out their own lived realities, in both reserve/ation and urban spaces. We should not place limits on the pluralisms and possibilities of being Indigenous in modern times. In other words, we should embrace the potential of hip hop culture.

Music has always been a part of Indigenous peoples' expressive culture and a part of their cultural and political sovereignty. Music has been crucial to Indigenous survival. Today, Indigenous music, especially hip hop, has served as an important part of Indigenous modernity and force for challenging settler colonialism. Shana Redmond writes that music is a method and that,

> Beyond its many pleasures, music allows us to do and imagine things that may otherwise be unimaginable or seem impossible. It is more than sound; it is a complex system of mean(ings) and ends that mediate our relationships to one another, to space, to our histories and historical moment.[50]

Redmond's use of music as an anthem for the African Diaspora is also true for Native people. It helps Native people imagine a future free from the strangling grip of colonialism and its effects. It is full of meanings that Native people can grasp onto in order to first imagine and then alter their futures, through hip hop.

Settler Colonialism

A note on settler colonialism is necessary here, as it is a defining feature of the everyday life of Native people. Patrick Wolfe might be one of the most important minds on settler colonialism. He writes, "Territoriality is settler colonialism's specific, irreducible element."[51] I agree here, and do not have much to add. The underlying component of settler colonialism is about gaining land. Missing from Wolfe's formulation, though, is the impact, both cultural and political, that settler colonialism has on

Native people. Therefore, I am compelled to rely on the work of Indigenous scholars to explain how it functions.

Yellow Knife Dené scholar Glen Coulthard provides more complex discussions of settler colonialism. For Coulthard, settler colonialism today, in addition to being about land dispossession, is also about recognition in a liberal paradigm. He argues that this current era of tribal communities seeking and gaining recognition from the state "in its contemporary liberal form promises to reproduce the very configurations of colonialist, racist, patriarchal state power that Indigenous peoples' demands for recognition."[52] Coulthard also explains the type of relationship that settler colonialism reproduces:

> A settler colonial relationship is one characterized by a particular form of domination, that is, it is a relationship whose power in this case, interrelated discursive and nondiscursive facets of economic, gendered, racial, and state power has been structured into a relatively secure or sedimented set of hierarchical social relations that continue to facilitate the dispossession of Indigenous peoples of their lands and self-determining authority.[53]

Coulthard takes settler colonialism to another level from Wolfe. He illustrates how race, gender, and state power all contribute to Indigenous dispossession. Of course, Indigenous dispossession is the major goal of a settler colonial state, but there are many ways in which this happens, and it is not outside of other social categories. Those are all important parts of understanding the process of settler colonialism and, at times, Native peoples' participation in those processes.

Chickasaw theorist Jodi Byrd writes that settler colonialism can be a transit, as well as a site through which to champion multiculturalism, or what people today call postracialism. On the former, Byrd writes, "as a transit, Indianness becomes a site through which US empire orients and replicates itself by transforming those to be colonized into 'Indians' through continual reiterations of pioneer logics, whether in the Pacific, the Caribbean, or the Middle East."[54] Byrd's brilliant use of using indigeneity as a transit allows us to understand how, historically and today, settler societies use their method for subjugating Indigenous histories and people as a mechanism through which to do the same to other marginalized people around the globe.

Second, the contemporary rhetoric of postracialism has dominated discourses during the presidency of Barack Obama. Perhaps most important for my purposes, is how Indianness is used in settler colonialism to control Native people and images, both literally and figuratively. "Images of American Indians in Western cultures, images that reify savageness and any 'primitiveness,'" writes Byrd, "rely upon emptying them of any tribal manifestation of identity, history, and culture, then filling them instead with those signifiers that assert mastery and control."[55] As Byrd identifies, these images are used to control Native bodies and also to ignore their contemporary realities. These are but two examples of the effects of settler colonialism.

Within a settler colonial state, Indigenous hip hop artists have a unique opportunity to raise the consciousness of Indigenous America to challenge colonialism in everyday forms. This should "continue to involve some form of critical individual and collective self-recognition on the part of Indigenous societies," writes Coulthard, "but with the understanding that our cultural practices have much to offer regarding the establishment of relationships within and between peoples and the natural world built on principle of reciprocity and respectful coexistence."[56] Native artists continue to challenge colonialism, and will continue to do so, raising consciousness, one performance and rhyme at a time.

Hip Hop Beats, Indigenous Rhymes is guided by at least three questions. First, how do Indigenous people construct indigeneity through hip hop culture? Second, in what ways does hip hop culture serve as a mechanism through which to construct sovereignty? Lastly, how does Indigenous peoples' engagement with and production of hip hop challenge mainstream stereotypes about Indigenous people as being relics of the past?

In order to answer these questions, this book will rely on several conceptual frameworks and methods to gather and analyze data. First, I will interview Native hip hop artists and ask them several questions that are centered on the themes of the book. I will choose these artists through snowball sampling and personal connections, hoping to get an equal representation in both tribal heritage(s) and gender(s). Second, I will collect data from a variety of sources. Because Indigenous hip hop is not very well known (in the mainstream sense), I will consult Indigenous media sources such as Indian Country Today Media Network, websites, as well as relying on the networks of artists that I have relationships with. I will analyze music, videos, and other forms of artistic expression in order to understand how race, gender, and indigeneity are constructed within hip hop. I am interested in forming a greater understanding of indigeneity as an analytic within Indigenous studies, as well as enhancing an already robust hip hop studies scholarship.

Organization of the Book

This book is not a comprehensive study of Indigenous hip hop culture. Instead, it is organized around the idea that Native artists in hip hop culture use a variety of methods to position themselves as modern people. The essays also highlight one of my intellectual interests: the intersections of blackness and indigeneity, which remains a marginalized subfield in both black and Indigenous studies. The essays in this book are thematic. That is, while they are connected by broader themes of Indigenous cultural representation, gender, and sovereignty as they manifest themselves through hip hop culture, they are still distinct. Ultimately, they are intellectual musings that I present here after presenting and conducting workshops from Toronto to Macon, Georgia, to the South Side of Chicago. There are six chapters total, the contents of which I explain below.

In chapter one, I argue that Native hip hop is a form of cultural sovereignty. Using Scott Richard Lyons's concept of Indigenous modernity and Michelle Raheja's concept of visual sovereignty, this chapter argues that Native artists not only challenge colonialism, but also offer a wide range of ideas for understanding the possibilities for imagining Indigenous future, where a great diversity of Native identities and expressive cultures can exist, with the overall goal of Indigenous sovereignty.

This chapter places Indigenous hip hop within the current political project of social movements in Canada and the United States, including #NativeLivesMatter, #NotYourMascot, Idle No More, and Walking With Our Sisters. Thus, Indigenous hip hop serves as the anthem for these movements for Indigenous sovereignty. This chapter also argues that Indigenous hip hop complements these social movements because it helps control the discourse of Native representation. This chapter also analyzes the premier of *Rebel Music: Native America*. Notably, it documents the importance of this mainstream representation, and why it matters for the future of disrupting Native stereotypes.

Chapter two analyzes Indigenous hip hop fashion. This chapter argues that Native people are carving out a niche within the hip hop community by wearing particular forms of Indigenous beadwork—what is called "Native bling"—and also adorning their bodies with tattoos, in order to highlight the variety of forms of Indigenous cultural expression. More than simply being a form of expression, Indigenous hip hop fashion serves as a cultural artifact, embedded with meaning and stories that allow Native people to assert their humanity in ways that directly confront the politics of colonialism. At the same time, Indigenous fashion must constantly fight against the colonial baggage of racist depictions. Some artists attempt to capitalize on these images, to varying degrees, still, with the ultimate goal of promoting Indigenous sovereignty.

Chapter three explores the competing notions of blackness and indigeneity within hip hop culture. While hip hop studies scholars have analyzed how whites have engaged in cultural appropriation, they have failed to examine how Indigenous hip hop artists—while not participating in cultural appropriation with a maliciousness of purpose, i.e., for commercial gain—do appropriate forms of blackness that contribute to its art. Similarly, scholars in Indigenous studies have analyzed how whites have engaged in cultural appropriation. This chapter complicates that narrative by arguing that it is neither this nor that, but somewhere in between, and we should acknowledge the complexities of hip hop culture, which allow for a range of artists to make it their own. Using black and Indigenous studies scholarship on black and Indigenous popular culture such as Mark Anthony Neal's concept of the post-soul aesthetic and Dean Rader's concept of "engaged resistance," this chapter argues for an Indigenous hip hop aesthetic that appreciates the uniqueness of both black American and Native American influences on Indigenous hip hop culture.

While Indigenous artists have a unique form of hip hop, we often forget that hip hop was formed as and remains a black cultural product (though there is some work that includes the Latinx influence in the foundational years). As a result, blackness cannot be erased from any form of Indigenous hip hop, especially in aesthetic, style, and language. This does not negate the uniqueness of Native hip hop. Instead, it expands the possibilities, and allows for scholars to more critically engage with the intersections of blackness and indigeneity, adding to the rich but often mundane scholarship of Afro-Indigenous studies.

Chapter four critically engages with how Native artists understand and construct gender within their art. Central to the chapter's theoretical foundation are Sam McKegney's *Masculindians: Conversations About Indigenous Manhood* (2014) and a variety of Native feminist scholars in developing a theory of gender in Indigenous hip hop culture. For example, this chapter analyzes the lyrics and images in Lakota rapper Frank Waln's "My Stone" video, which I read as an example of how Indigenous feminism can inform and help reconstruct Indigenous masculinity.

At the same time, in keeping with the idea that Native people are modern subjects, and hoping to avoid re-stereotyping how Native people are *supposed* to behave, I discuss the not-so-flattering picture of Native hip hop artists who do not necessarily promote a progressive view of gender in some of their work. Thus, this chapter complicates ideas of what Native gender(s) looks like in hip hop culture, and thereby avoids the many pitfalls of scholarship that focus only on the "positive" representations of Indigenous expressive culture.

In chapter five, I take an unconventional approach by presenting an interview that I did with Sicangu Lakota hip hop artist Frank Waln. While it might be conventional to critically analyze the interview, Frank and I have a prior working relationship, and I wanted to share with others his thoughts and ideas about what we have previously discussed. We cover the broader ideas of colonialism, race, gender, and black-Indigenous relations, and how all that plays out in his music and in his role as a hip hop artist/intellectual.

I end *Hip Hop Beats, Indigenous Rhymes* by restating the major arguments of the book, and concluding that Indigenous hip hop is, through cultural expression, an assertion of Indigenous sovereignty. Unique in its form and structure, this conclusion argues that Indigenous hip hop can play a major role in challenging settler colonialism. It also argues that Indigenous hip hop presents another way that Native people can continue to challenge stereotypes about them, and not be bound by the "colonial politics of recognition" of both their home communities and mainstream society. I also end by suggesting ways that the Indigenous hip hop generation might take action to deal with particular issues within the Indigenous world.

Finally, I want to stress that Indigenous hip hop artists are engaged in what Mohawk scholar Audra Simpson calls "the act of refusal." Though writing about how Mohawk people disrupt the settler states of Canada and the United States by their presence and actions, her thoughts on refusal are also useful for describing contemporary Indigenous hip hop artists. As Simpson writes, "their political consciousness and actions upend the perception that colonization, elimination, and settlement are situations of the past."[57] Hip hop artists do this through their lyrics by literally and simply *being* Native hip hop artists. She continues, "they have not let go of themselves or their traditions, and they subvert this requirement at every turn with their actions."[58] Regardless of what we might think of their lyrics or whether they are "progressive" or not, they refuse to be boxed into stereotypes. Their performance as Native artists suggests that Native people can continue to be themselves, and to be living, breathing subjects engaged squarely in modernity.

Chapter One

#NOTYOURMASCOT

Indigenous Hip Hop Artists
as Modern Subjects

The #NotYourMascot hashtag is a social media activist response to mascot names like the Washington R*dsk*ns team in Washington, D.C., and the Cleveland I*di*ns. Led by activists such as Amanda Blackhorse, it is very important that they challenge this colonial manifestation. Equally important is that their message is clear: We are products of contemporary times, not stuck in some historical time machine in which we simply cannot become modern. They are embracing Indigenous modernity.

To embrace the manifestations of contemporary Indigenous popular cultures such as hip hop on their *own* terms is to also embrace Indigenous modernity. By modernity, I am taking a simple but complex definition put forward by Scott Richard Lyons. He writes, "To embrace indigenous modernity is to usher in other modern concepts . . . including the concepts of decolonization."[1] Decolonization itself has varying definitions, but one of my favorites is put forth by decolonial theorist Frantz Fanon. He writes, "In its bare reality, decolonization reeks of red-hot cannonballs and bloody knives. For the last can be first only after a murderous and decisive confrontation between the two protagonists."[2] I am not advocating the use of violence for radical social change, per se, but I am calling Indigenous hip hop artists warriors, armed with both words and art. This art can, in turn, get people—especially the seventh generation—moving to change their existing social conditions. But I also conceptualize Indigenous hip hop as an art form with a variety of representations and styles.

Now, back to Lyons. By Indigenous modernity, I understand him to mean to accept things that are new, and which are different from times past. Lyons further states that "an embracement of indigenous modernity requires a different relationship to the past, one that does not seek to go backward but instead attempts to bring the past forward."[3] Different in this case does not mean an abandonment of tradition or better than something previous; it simply means that we live in a different epoch, which requires different ways of knowing and living—ways of being and knowing in the world that are informed by our ancestors but not in such a way that makes us relics of the past, participating in the colonial imagination constructed by settlers.

It also means acknowledging that Indigenous persons can remix their realities in ways that make sense to them, based upon the material world around them. Too often, scholars and community folks throw around words like "traditional" in an attempt to connect the past and present and thereby espouse some imaginary, unattainable form of Indigenous authenticity. I think some sincerely desire to pass on teachings that have continued in spite of settlers' attempts at erasing an Indigenous identity in the United States and in other settler states. Oftentimes, though, we become stuck in the exact binary in which settlers wanted us to be. Settlers are modern while Indigenous people are relics of the past, unable to attain said modernity; the end result is the continuation of the very binary the settlers created. While I do not think it desirable to assimilate—and how and what that means for Indigenous people in particular contexts is complicated and never neutral—we should not fear the embracement of Indigenous modernity, or, in this case, Indigenous hip hop.

With that being said, it is not useful to embrace certain products of Western modernity, including colonialism, imperialism, patriarchy, racism, sexism, and so forth. Still, we can embrace certain components and, in the spirit of hip hop ingenuity, remix them into something different. After all, while we are products *of* colonialism, we should not become bound *to* it.

Hip hop, and I mean all forms of it, should be allowed to thrive within Indigenous communities, as they are, until we come to a point where we can change the social conditions around us. For example, I do not think it is useful or even desirable to apply the label "traditional" or "conscious" to Indigenous hip hop. Indigenous hip hop may be a distinct thing in origin and, at times, content and form that includes rhyme schemes and aesthetics. However, its uniqueness should not be tied to things of the past, or what some may call "authentic." We should not value one form of Indigenous hip hop over another just because the artists use "traditional" teachings or rap in Indigenous languages. Nor should we gravitate toward the idea that hip hop is almost exclusively useful only for fitting specific political agendas. (I'm thinking here of the old debate between W. E. B. Du Bois and Langston Hughes. The former argued that art was useful only if it served as political propaganda, while the latter argued that we should appreciate art for art's sake. I'm probably in the middle on this, perhaps leaning at one moment to the Du Boisian camp and at another to Hughes. In sum, it is all contextual.)

To be clear, I do think there is a place for hip hop serving as a political tool within Indigenous communities. For instance, we know that Indigenous languages and stories are not easily translated into the English language.[4] In this context and place, hip hop serving as a political tool within Indigenous communities is great, and it can be used to help revitalize languages and pass on stories. At the same time, Native people have always adapted to whatever situation they have found themselves in, whether good or bad. In other words, Indigenous peoples' engagement with hip hop should operate under the assumption of plurality, not singularity.

Framing Indigenous hip hop within the context of Indigenous modernity has great potential. As my homie and South Side Chicago poet J. Ivy says, "They say the sky's the limit, but I now believe that space is the limit, and space is limitless."[5] Indigenous hip hop has limitless potential, and I want to explicate on that. Before turning to examples of contemporary manifestations of Indigenous modernity and hip hop, let me offer a brief history of Indigenous hip hop.

Indigenous Hip Hop: A Very Brief History

If you talked to a variety of Indigenous hip hop heads, they would give you many different comments about where hip hop emerged. But for the sake of argument, I will refer to the published dissertation of Aaron Aquallo. He argues that Native hip hop emerged in the late 1980s, right alongside West Coast hip hop and gangsta rap. Specifically, Aquallo highlights two major parties involved in the development of US Native hip hop: WithOUT Rezervation (WOR) and Paul Gary Davis, or Litefoot in the Bay Area and Long Beach.[6] He writes, "WOR captured the energy and spirit of West Coast Hip Hop transposing this sub genre through multiple tribal influences. As a result, Native Hip Hop arrived as a presence within the dynamic national and global Hip Hop culture."[7] The uniqueness of this story is that WOR participated in the Intertribal Friendship House in Oakland, California, notably an urban area with a long history of postwar Indigenous activism.[8] While Aquallo does delve into the history of Indigenous activism in North America, a word on Native activism in postwar America is important to acknowledge. I will begin with the red power movement.

The red power movement rapidly swept across Indian country. Beginning at least since the American Indian movement's 1968 formation in Minneapolis, Minnesota, the red power movement sparked a major turn in US–Indigenous relations.[9] The 1970s marked a complete reversal in US policies toward American Indians, from termination to self-determination. Due to Native activism, Indian self-determination was translated into law, culminating in the passage of the Indian Self-Determination and Education Act of 1975. Generally, this act sought to begin the process of empowering Indian peoples to solve Indian problems. The 1980s saw the beginning of change for some Native communities,[10] even as the conservative backlash was implanted due to neoliberalism and Reaganomics.[11] Today, Native people, at least in the United States, still operate under the idea of self-determination. Whether or not it actually works depends on what Native nation you speak with, but sovereignty and determining their own futures remains a deeply important rhetorical and political ideal of Native nations today. Hip hop as a cultural art form has a role in these conversations. I will now turn to an analysis of an episode of the MTV documentary *Rebel Music*, which aired in November 2014.

Indigenous Hip Hop Goes Mainstream:
MTV's Rebel Music: Native America

I, along with many Indigenous people, waited with enthusiasm for the November 2014 premiere of the MTV documentary *Rebel Music: Native America: 7th Generation Rises.* In a renewed moment of Indigenous activism in North America, seeing the nationally televised documentary, especially the combination of hip hop and Indigenous activism, was truly a historic event.

The entire board consisted of Indigenous people, ranging from Cherokee to Esselen/Ohlone, from both Canada and the US. In a time when Indigenous people were (and are) challenging colonialism in a variety of ways, including through social media and film, they helped contribute to that struggle by showcasing contemporary artists who were not bound by settler imaginaries. There are many hip hop–themed documentaries of the culture itself and individual artists, but this was the first Indigenous one.

Melissa Leal, an Esselen/Ohlone scholar of Indigenous hip hop, played a significant role in the development of the project. (I saw her present at the 2015 Native American and Indigenous Studies Association annual meeting in Washington, D.C.) She has a degree in Native American studies from the University of California at Davis, and currently works at the Indian Education Program in the Elk Grove Unified School District in Northern California.[12] She shared her story about the project's development and how they brought it into fruition. What I recall most about her discussion of the project is that she wanted to avoid stereotypes of Native people. This is an admirable thing but one that is difficult to determine or control, given that stereotypical representations of Indigenous people are endemic to settler societies.

The documentary features artists Frank Waln (Sicangu Lakota), Inez Jasper (Kole First Nation), Nataanii Means (Dakota, Diné, Oglala Lakota), and Mike "Witko" Cliff (Oglala Lakota). They cover issues of youth suicide, the activism against the construction of the Keystone Pipeline through Indian country, the missing and murdered Indigenous women, the #NativeLivesMatter movement, and how those issues influenced their art. Frank Waln argues, "I definitely think there's a connection between traditional storytelling and hip hop. My people have been storytellers for thousands of years, and this is just a new way to tell our stories." This is a powerful point. Indigenous artists' engagement with hip hop culture illustrates that they are informed by history but not confined to it.

The documentary, though, is not only about hip hop. Its portrayal of the struggles of Native people on reserve/ations, and the connection of those struggles to hip hop, is commendable. Those challenges include the many missing and murdered Indigenous women in Canada, youth suicide, and police brutality. As Inez Jasper suggests, "[I]t's the system that's to blame, and the system needs to take responsibility."

Although the production was great and the music excellent, there are at least three lingering questions for the documentary. First, what is the history of Indigenous hip hop in North America? There are more than a few hip hop history texts, but we still know very little about the origins of hip hop in Indigenous North America. While we want to show that Native people are products of the present—perhaps we might call this modernity—we cannot overlook that history.

Second, how does urban space influence these artists? We know that, today, in both the US and Canada, the majority of Native people live in cities. And yet there was no discussion of the importance of urban space and how that contributed to these artists' development. Yes, they come from reserve/ation communities, but they are also influenced by other spaces. If hip hop is anything, it is tied to the urban, and there are several urban scenes in the documentary. In fact, the artists attended a climate change march *and* recorded some dope songs together in New York City—the cradle of hip hop culture.

Finally, what is the link between blackness and indigeneity? It is difficult to understand any form of hip hop without a clear discussion of blackness. Indigenous hip hop presents an opportunity to examine the intersections of blackness and indigeneity that remain narrowly confined to certain academic subjects. For instance, while Cliff is speaking to youth on his rez, one cannot help but notice that he is wearing a tee shirt that has the late Notorious BIG's album cover *Ready to Die* (1994) on the front. What is it about Christopher Wallace that Cliff might be able to identify with? Perhaps it is the ubiquitous presence of death that is always in the awareness of black and Indigenous men.

A Commentary on the Curriculum

To make this documentary accessible for teachers, Kate Jorgensen and Melissa Leal created a curriculum to accompany the project. The curriculum is designed to correspond to the Common Core curriculum in the United States, specifically the English language arts/literacy and social studies Common Core state standards. Grades 9–10 and 11–12 are the target audience. Eighteen pages total, it is broken down by goals and audience, and tips for lesson plans. The document is a powerful example of how Native people are challenging colonial representations through education.[13]

The goals of the lesson plan are straightforward, and premised on one broad question: How do we understand the complex history of North America? The lesson plan is designed to,

> . . . help students build a deeper understanding of Native American history and contemporary and historical issues that influence indigenous communities in the United States and Canada by examining the powerful narratives of youth, analyzing various texts, and making connections to their personal experiences.[14]

While they provide this lesson plan, Jorgensen and Leal are quick to point out that the lessons should be used with "flexibility" and should be open to modifications. The authors begin the guide by explaining where each of the artists are from; the places include the Rosebud Reservation, represented by Frank Waln; the Pine Ridge Reservation, represented by Mike Cliff and Nataanii Means; and Chilliwack, British Columbia, Canada, the home of the Skowkale First Nation, represented by Inez Jasper. Altogether they offer some unique representations of Native people throughout North America.

The first section tells a brief story about the Rosebud Sioux Reservation in South Dakota. It explains a brief history of the development of the reservation, and offers a contemporary look at the demographics. It highlights the specific group, the Sicangu Lakota. A unique detail that they cite is that one-third of the Rosebud population lives off the reservation in urban areas.

The second section is a brief window into the past and present of the Pine Ridge Reservation in South Dakota. It highlights the geographic location of that reservation; it then discusses the social issues on the reservation, including the 75 percent of adults who suffer from alcoholism. They also highlight the 80 percent unemployment rate and that 49 percent of people live below the poverty line. The history of Pine Ridge offers some of the most infamous moments of violence and resistance in Native American history. In 1890, a fellow Lakota officer killed Sitting Bull; and, in December 1890, the US Calvary murdered children, women, and men. Later, in the 1970s, Pine Ridge and its citizens were often the source of activism, including the occupation of Wounded Knee.

The authors offer us a window into the Skowkale, who are members of the Sto:lo Nation and are located in Chilliwack, British Columbia. They give a brief history of how that nation, in its modern iteration, came to be. They also do an excellent job of illustrating some of the cultural activities that many in the Pacific Northwest continue to do.

Explaining the history of these places is important for students, especially non-Indigenous students, so that they gain at least a rudimentary conception of how Native communities and land came to be, and how they look today. These brief explanations can easily lead to students further exploring the histories of these people and others, with a guide from teachers.

While the other information is readily available and useful, perhaps the major accomplishment of this curriculum is the section titled "Missing and Murdered Aboriginal Women and Violence Against Women." They begin by highlighting the report commissioned by the Royal Canadian Mounted Police in Canada, in which they confirmed that there were nearly 1,200 cases of violence against women over the last thirty years.

They also highlight that, in the United States, Indigenous women are more than 2.5 times more likely to be sexually assaulted than any other racial group. Related to that, non-Indigenous men commit about 80 percent of those sexual assaults. Importantly, they highlight that President Obama reauthorized the Violence Against Women Act, which will afford a few tribes the power to prosecute non-Native men for abuse and sexual assault. I would imagine that this curriculum could go a long way for not only young women, but also lead into an important discussion for young men about sexual assault and abuse against women (and those who have multiple gender identities).

They also offer context lessons. These are detailed accounts about how they fit into Common Core state standards. The first lesson is about poverty on Native American reservations, specifically Pine Ridge. The second lesson is on Native American suicide. The final lessons consist of allowing students to learn of stories from the Pine Ridge Reservation.

Taken together, this curriculum is a wonderful starting point, and will hopefully be an important contribution to the study of Native peoples in a contemporary fashion. Indeed, it has the potential to challenge the notion of Indigenous invisibility, and get students to understand the historical relationship between Native nations and the government of the United States (and Canada). That notwithstanding, this curriculum is a start (and an exceptional one). It suffers from at least two flaws, which are larger issues in Native American and Indigenous studies. First, the urban is not highlighted in the manner it should be, which I briefly mentioned regarding the documentary. Second, we have to wonder how much this curriculum will do to actually challenge students to see the great diversity of Native America.

As a trained historian of urban Indigenous history, I notice it immediately. The only mention of urban is when they paraphrase the population of the Rosebud Lakota, one-third of which live off of the reservation in urban areas. In our quest to challenge stereotypes about Native people, including where they live, we must ask: How do we discuss First Nations people in a way that represents the diverse experiences that they have? While the mention of these perspectives is to highlight the role of

Native people in the documentary, they also now do a lot of work and live in urban areas.

This brilliant documentary is timely, necessary, and a welcome contribution to Indigenous popular cultural studies, Indigenous studies, hip hop studies, and the public. Yet, we need more. Hopefully *Rebel Music: Native America* is the beginning of a host of works that explore the importance and usefulness of hip hop as a modern expression of sovereignty. These artists also inspire. As Mike Cliff states, "My ancestors fought and died for me to even be alive. I have a responsibility. If we don't pick up that fight, who will?" Indigenous hip hop artists might very well be the warriors of the twenty-first century.

First Out Here: Indigenous Hip Hop

I did a workshop at an R1 research university during Black History Month in 2016. The topic was on black and Indigenous relations in contemporary popular culture. I showed Beyonce's "Formation," and played Frank Waln's "What Makes the Red Man Red." Many students came up to me proclaiming that they had a good time and learned a lot. One young person stated, "that was the most woke program we've had here in a minute." A few tried to argue with me about my swearing and how it negatively impacted their ability to learn bless their hearts.

Most memorable for me was a Latinx student who came up to me and asked if I had seen a documentary about Indigenous hip hop in Canada, and whether it was legit. I had not. The student subsequently sent me two separate emails asking if I had seen it yet. Though I planned to, the urgency pushed me to take a peek at it earlier than I had anticipated. Although only twenty-five minutes long, I was not disappointed. Big shout out to that student for suggesting it to me.

Published on YouTube on January 21, 2016, *First Out Here Indigenous Hip Hop in Canada* is hosted by Ritchie Acheampong (Rich Kidd), a Toronto-born hip hop artist known for his production and rapping. The documentary analyzes the experiences of Indigenous artists in four Canadian cities: Regina, Saskatchewan; Winnipeg, Manitoba; Edmonton,

Alberta; and the place I would love to claim as my second home, T Dot (Toronto), Ontario. Although male-centric, it reveals the tensions between "tradition" and "modernity," and how Native artists struggle to deal with that complex scenario. The artists struggle to deal with this not only within the context of their own Indigenous and non-Indigenous people, but within themselves.

Although several artists are included, only a few are featured. The first is Drezus, whose other name is Jeremiah Manitopyes, a Plains Cree artist from Regina. The second artist is Tommay Da, also from Regina. Drezus is the main subject in Regina. Like many Native people who grow up in cities, he felt stigmatized by other Native people who grew up on the reserve. Rich Kidd asks him, "How do you find a way to mesh today's kinda modern music with your traditional culture?" Drezus responds,

> My whole life I think I've been trying to do that, in my life. You know what I mean? I was always looked at as an outsider from the people from the reserve. City boy, this and that, I don't know shit about the land. But I'm taking those steps to learn the culture, right. So, my whole life, I had these two different sides. So, with my music, it reflects that.

As Drezus articulates here, they, like other Native people, are dealing with the contradictions of modernity and its impact on Native people in the Western imagination: being invisible. As I have articulated elsewhere, Native invisibility is a part of the larger process of dispossession. To continue settler colonialism, one must also consistently state that Native people are invisible. Drezus attempts to reconcile these seeming contradictions between "traditional" life and modern expressions of Native people.

Native rappers are a microcosm to understanding Native people in general; they are invisible to the outside world. When Rich Kidd asks Drezus if he thinks Indigenous hip hop will ever go mainstream, he responds, "I don't think we get the respect we deserve as a people, first of all." Drezus's flipping of Indigenous peoples' position in mainstream (Canadian) society is a significant reminder about how colonialism works for Native people: they are rendered invisible. He continues, "In order for us to grow as hip hop artists, we need that community support fully, from our own people." He is not asking for mainstream validation; rather, he seeks the recognition from his own people. His major reason for doing this is to try and build a community to break down the misconceptions about hip hop culture and its potential role in creating a decolonial future.

There is also a moment in the film in which Drezus, Rich Kidd, and and Helen Matechuck, Drezus's *kokum* (which is "grandmother" in Cree) are seen sitting together. There is a park in the background, and they are sitting on two connected benches with Helen in the middle, Rich Kidd on her right, and Drezus on her left. She says she's "proud of Jeremiah." Rich Kidd asks Helen about life on the reserve. She pauses, reflecting, then says, "It was pretty rough, but we survived through it. We went to residential, it's a hard story. I couldn't speak my language. Every time I tried they slapped me on the side of the head." This is, unfortunately, a common story among residential school survivors.

In Canada, there is a current dialogue regarding the Truth and Reconciliation Commission. It is supposed to bring healing and to reconcile the abuse and damage these schools caused to generations of First Nations people (and elsewhere where Indigenous people exist). You can see the pain in Helen's eyes as she reflects on what happened to her. Rich Kidd then asks Drezus, "How do you feel Kokum Helen influences your music?" He responds,

> She's like a source of strength for me. She made it this far; she has this whole family who loves her, who looks up to her. Like, I wanna be there, I wanna be that person for my family. For her to make it through all that stuff that she went through, in residential school and especially Regina where it's a lot of racism, tons of racism, it's in your face, slap-you-in-the-face-type racism, you know, she's definitely a source of strength.

Older mother and grandmother figures have generally served as inspiration for male hip hop artists. For example, we can recall hip hop legend Tupac Shakur's track "Dear Mama" as an anthem expressing his difficult relationship with his mother, but ultimately his deep and everlasting love for her and all the struggles they have dealt with. But the contradiction lies in how male rappers represent Native women, often in a misogynist tone, while at the same time expressing their love for their mothers, sisters, aunts, and daughters. Regardless, the inspiration that Drezus garners from his grandmother's stories is well worth highlighting. It might serve to help other Indigenous men to reconcile the contradiction of producing sexist lyrics and imagery while expressing their love for women. It may also help them begin to engage more fully with Indigenous feminist approaches to building relationships, through the stories of their relatives and hopefully, also, nonrelatives, for an oppression-free future.

The only female emcee mentioned very briefly is an aspiring artist named T-Rhyme. She came to Winnipeg for the first time as part of Aboriginal Music Week in Winnipeg, along with Drezus and the Winnipeg Boyz. With Drezus as a mentor, she is slowly emerging as an Indigenous voice to be reckoned with. Rich Kidd asks her, "What is the subject matter and content in your lyrics?" She replies, "I'm gonna be focusing more on issues of like, the missing and murdered women, and basically storytelling of my experiences." When asked about the missing and murdered women, she responds, "It definitely makes me feel uneasy, in the sense that, I know my worth, for somebody else to devalue who I am based just on the color of my skin, I don't want to be seen as any less than the next person." Unfortunately, a lot of her work is not featured in the piece; part of the reason for that, perhaps, is that her work is only just now being discovered. However, it does shed light on the lack of coverage of Indigenous female emcees, and why their voices can by silenced by male-centric narratives.

Rich Kidd also travels to Winnipeg and meets rap duo the Winnipeg Boyz, which includes Jon-C and Charlie Fettah. (They were formerly Winnipeg's Most, which included Brooklyn, who died in September 2015.) Winnipeg is the city in Manitoba with the largest First Nations population. In the documentary, Rich Kidd travels there and meets the rap duo, where they share their stories about growing up in Winnipeg. He asks them to describe the unique things that Native artists bring to the hip hop scene. Fettah responds, "I think it's opening up people's eyes to a lot of stuff they don't know. Systemic racism." Jon-C follows up with a comment about the idea of Native invisibility: "People think we extinct. People think we extinct. You ask people in the States and they think we live in igloos up here. It's messed up." Fettah follows that up with specific examples of what he and Jon-C try to expose others to in their music:

> We can talk the real shit, the gangster's love. Let's talk about the fucked-up shit that's really going on in our city. The missing and murdered women, the kids that are growing up with nothing, and I mean literally nothing. I'm working at parks and these kids ain' got no fuckin' shoes. And not because they lost them; you can tell.

Jon-C exposes the poverty of First Nations people in Winnipeg. According to the Canadian Centre for Policy Alternatives and Save the Children Canada report, 62 percent of First Nations children lived in poverty.[15]

To deal with childhood poverty and the lack of resources, Fettah started a program called Mic Check, where Native youth can drop on in and record their music. They provide free studio time, as well as mentoring. This is the type of program that Native youth in Canada need, and it is a creative way to use hip hop to express oneself in a beautiful way, through rapping.

Between Modernity and Tradition

Another artist featured in the documentary is David "Gordo" Strickland, who has served as a sound engineer on many projects, including Toronto hip hop superstar Drake's 2012 award-winning album, *Take Care*. He also worked on Wu Tang member Method Man's album *4:21...The Day After*, including the track "Say," which features hip hop legend Lauryn Hill. Rich Kidd goes to Strickland's house, and they spend a significant amount of time discussing Strickland's struggles growing up in Scarborough, a diverse area of eastern Toronto.

Because of Toronto's diversity, growing up, he did not really recognize that he was Indigenous. It was not until his adulthood that he began to identify more carefully with being Native. Though some Indigenous folks may believe that hip hop is not the best medium through which to express Indigenous cultures, Strickland breaks it down, saying that the spirit of hip hop has always been there. Or conversely, we might say that the spirit of indigeneity has been there since the formation of hip hop. His metaphoric reasoning is simple: the drummer serves as the deejay, the singers and storytellers are the rappers. Thus, we see the collision of modernity and "tradition" easily adapted for contemporary times.

Strickland expresses that he did not grow up with his "traditional" Indigenous culture. However, he has recently attempted to reconnect with his Native roots, including engaging in sweat ceremonies. He also smudges to cleanse his heart, mind, and spirit. Still, he remains deeply engaged with the Toronto hip hop scene. He believes that Native hip hop will go mainstream. As he explains, "You're starting to see, not only do we have scene, but we have quality artists emerging and building. And, you know, more than a few now. We're getting that type of qualities coming to the forefront." This seems to be the case. When Rich Kidd follows up by asking him specifically, "So, do you feel like some of these artists on the verge of a brink, like, basically mainstream success?" Strickland responds, "As long as we keep pushing, it's bound to happen." He suggests that so long as Native people keep producing good quality music, it is bound to happen. "We've had some close, close encounters, but, you know, we just gotta keep pushing as artists."

In the following scene, the documentary introduces us to rapper Que Rock, with whom Strickland worked. Que Rock is an Anishinaabe from Nippising First Nation. He does all four elements of hip hop.[16] While he asserts his identity as an Indigenous person, he does not believe that Native hip hop should necessarily be labeled as such. Instead, he produces an interesting narrative seeking inclusion into the larger culture of hip hop.

Rich Kidd asks Que Rock, "Do you think Native artists are getting the respect that they deserve yet, or do you think it still has a long ways to go before they reach mainstream status?" Que Rock responds, "I don't ever put myself into the category of saying 'Native hip hop' because there's no such thing." This response is interesting. He maintains an Indigenous identity but does not necessarily want to be known as an Indigenous artist. It presents an understandable conundrum. Perhaps seeking mainstream hip hop validation would allow him to move beyond the stereotypes associated with being Indigenous. On the other hand, it could also maintain a key part of contemporary Indigenous existence: invisibility. He argues, through an Indigenous example, why he uses this line of thinking, "Whoever, like, comes to the drum that you're playing, those are your people. There's no color to that; that's hip hop. So I love to see Native artists look at the world standard, you know what I mean, and go by that standard." Given that hip hop has gone global, it is difficult to conceptualize what the "world standard" of the medium is. If he simply means that hip hop crosses cultures, state-created borders, and ethnicities and races, that is absolutely true. His example of the drum is useful because it allows us to see that some Native people—and I believe Indigenous hip hop artists are unique to that—are inclusive, at least when it comes to skin color.

Unfortunately, this narrative erases the unique cultures and identities that any particular group, in this case Native people, adds to hip hop. I do not believe that Indigenous hip hop artists have to produce hyper-representations of indigeneity in their work, nor should they be required to discuss what it means to be Native in some capacity. And while it is important to introduce the world to contemporary Native life, I also believe that this narrative borders on contributing to the multicultural logic of celebrating our diversity, which then renders our important differences unimportant. This line of thinking also fails to recognize the material conditions that First Nations people face in Canada compared to their white counterparts. Furthermore, it erases the particular black cultural elements of hip hop that have moved into Native communities, even as it has become its own cultural artifact. If Que Rock ultimately seeks an idealistic Indigenous future free of colonialism and gender violence, his point holds true. However, we are not at a point where we can all be hip hop heads and ignore our unique Indigenous cultures and identities.

This documentary serves as an important contribution to our understanding of contemporary Indigenous life in Canada through the medium of hip hop. While male-centric, it at least shows Native people as modern subjects in North America, challenging colonial ideas of Indigenous invisibility, through hip hop culture. Like Strickland, I am hoping Indigenous hip hop in Canada and the United States will become mainstream to the point where white America (in Canada and the US) respects Native people as human beings. The danger, though, lies in what could happen if Native artists do go mainstream. Will their cultures be erased? Will white Americans love the artists but continue discriminating against everyday First Nations people? Time will tell. But there is hope.

Supaman, the "Prayer Loop Song," and the Politics of Authenticity

I remember when Supaman's "Prayer Loop Song" went viral. I was deeply engaged in research on my dissertation in Detroit. In fact, I was at a coffee shop right on Woodward Avenue, struggling to write a chapter of my dissertation on Indigenous women in postwar Detroit. Then, this song came across my Facebook newsfeed and it gave me the motivation I needed to put some scribbles on the page.

Admittedly, I was drawn first to the aesthetics of the video, which I shall describe later. Then, I searched through the YouTube comments section (almost always a mistake, I know!); someone basically said that they liked it until the message got all preachy. Then I decided to listen more carefully to the lyrics. Sure enough, it had a very positive, explicitly Christian message. I thought it was dope. But searching further on other Native blogs and websites revealed that, while many appreciated Supaman's art, others found it a challenge to listen to because it was not Native enough, or authentic. In this section, I will describe the video and engage with ideas of authenticity.

Christian Parrish Takes the Gun, better known by his stage name Supaman, is a Crow rapper from Montana. Both of his parents were alcoholics, and he spent many years as a child in foster care, until his grandfather took him in. In an interview with NPR, he stated that he had been listening to hip hop since he was young. After engaging in a life of crime early on, he began rapping and touring. After searching and struggling for meaning in his life in spite of hip hop culture, he says he picked up a Bible and just started praying. He walked away from his record deal and went back to the rez. Some liked his new lyrics about God, while others hated them. Still, he pressed on.[17]

Supaman, while being an Indigenous rapper, is also a Christian rapper, infusing both parts of his identity into his music. Perhaps the most notable example of that is his performance of the "Prayer Loop Song," which has over a million views since being uploaded to YouTube in 2014. The song is the quintessential demonstration of the combination of the four hip hop elements, Indigenous modernity, and cultural infusion. In the video, he is in Billings Gazette's Studio in Billings, Montana. He is wearing his regalia. The first frame begins with a zoom-in on a boom box. He begins by drumming, turns on the boom box, uses the flute, starts a bit of robot, then he starts beatboxing, then uses some tonal singing, which is a part of powwow music. He then starts deejayin'— scratching a vinyl with powwow music. He spits his verse, and then he starts break-dancing, infusing what seems to be a mix of fancy dancing and break-dancing.

The verse is short, but it is a message of prayer, hoping to uplift a broad Native community. It is explicitly Christian in its message:

I pray for the ones listening right now
Struggling/feel like givin' in right now
I pray for you/pray that you come back home
I pray that you'll understand that you're never alone
I pray for the single mothers and the deadbeat dads
Drop their kids off and go party gets me mad
So, I pray, pray for peace then pray for change
Keep on prayin' when everything stays the same
And I pray for the pastors and all of the churches
And those who cry light songs on following hearses
I pray for you
Pray for the sick and the poor
Pray for the rich man who don't give to the lord
And I pray for wisdom and I pray for power and
I pray we'll be ready in the final hour
I pray for those who keep judging men in the streets
And I pray for my friends and enemies.

The lyrics are pretty straightforward, and I don't think they require much analysis. He is praying for those in terrible conditions, the poor, and he simply wants a better life for those in need, both materially and spiritually. I think any person with a conscience can't hate on these lyrics too badly. However, responses to them and the video do require analysis.

The responses to the song on blogs and websites are fascinating. While the majority are showin' love to Supaman, appreciating his powerful message and words of encouragement for those who might feel downtrodden, others were straight hatin'. While it is difficult to know whether or not these are Native people, let alone what community they come from, it is a common critique: that using rap and hip hop somehow makes his message less "authentically" Native. Read in another way, it is straight-up antiblack. Check out one of the comments from someone named Arlinda J: "Please do not incorporate rap into traditional native music. Our song are prayers, like your video, and I'm sure you will go a long way. So good luck with your career. Keep our traditions and native cultures where they belong. Respect our ways."[18]

On the one hand, this person, Native or non-Native, is engaging in the discourse of authenticity, suggesting that there is a pure form of Native culture and way of living. That is an old argument when Native people, in modern times, have incorporated other non-Native peoples' cultures into their own. (This makes me wonder whether, prior to European contact, Native communities responded the same way when a Native person brought in other cultural elements of other Native folks? Hmmmm.) Second, this person is suggesting that the fusion of one cultural form of expression—hip hop—and Native music is a violation of Native traditions. It also reeks of the conservative idea that some in the black church may have about Christian rap music and rap music in general.[19]

Let me offer a deeper reading of this: it suggests that a black cultural art form is, in fact, diluting Native purity. In other words, this person is engaging with a form of antiblackness. Roll with my logic for a minute. It is not to say that all Native people are racist or hate black folks; nor am I trying to engage in the "politics of the oppression" Olympics, saying that one group has it harder. My point here is that underneath this comment, which is historically rooted, there is a sentiment of antiblackness, but with a specific focus on hip hop. It is a form of racism without racists.[20]

It is unfortunate that such perspectives exist, especially for an artist trying to uplift his community in the best way possible. As Scott Richard Lyons suggests, we should not focus on what an "authentic" Indigenous person is; instead, "we should ask what kinds of Indian identities are in production during a given historical moment and what is at stake in their meaning."[21] Supaman in particular and hip hop artists in general can help us delve into this conversation in productive ways. I still have some hope that we can get past these times of wastefulness in which we focus so much on authenticity. Regardless, we should give Supaman mad props, whether Christian or non-Christian, for sharing with us his art and his message.

From Red Power to Hip Hop

Nataanii Means is the son of an American Indian movement legend and activist, the late Russell Means. He remains a controversial figure from the red power movement; some revere(d) him, some hate(d) him. His star shined so brightly that in 1992 Hollywood called, and he was a costar in *The Last of the Mohicans*, the James Fenimore Cooper book adapted for the big screen, also starring Daniel Day-Lewis.

Nataanii takes on the warrior spirit of his father through rap music. He is a warrior without weapons, fighting against colonialism in the twenty-first century. He explicitly connects the red power movement with today's Indigenous struggle for change. He was never more on point in this effort than with the track "The Radical," from his 2013 album *2 Worlds*. What does the word "radical" mean? In the Frantz Fanonian sense, it means to get at the root of something. For Indigenous communities in particular, it means to find ways of challenging the power of colonialism. Nataanii's father, Russell, did this through direct action and disruption; Nataanii does it through hip hop culture.

It is also a song about warriorhood, or Indigenous masculinity. Back in Russell Means's day, he said that, when first meeting Dennis Banks and seeing them disrupt a meeting of church members in Detroit, he remarked, "A whole week in Detroit with AIM had changed my whole outlook."[22] In what way did it change his outlook? He wrote, "For the first time, I knew the purpose of my life and the path I must follow to fulfill it. A the age of thirty I became full-time Indian."[23] AIM's aggressive, even masculine activist tactics appealed to Russell Means on a personal level. It reinvigorated his wish to be an Indian, an Indian man. And as history has told us, he continued in that path, by any means necessary.

Nataanii followed in a similar path, only through hip hop. He can become masculine, reenacting for today's audience red power's idea of Indigenous masculinity by rapping. The video "The Radical" tells this story. This track and video is a break from the beneficial, but often over-gloried, time of Indigenous protest.

The video begins with a mural of graffiti in the background. The painter/tagger is high on a ladder, while Nataanii walks into the scene. The tagger has a roller dripping with red paint, symbolizing, perhaps, the blood of his ancestors. Nataanii walks in wearing a hoodie emblazoned with the face of the epitome of Indigenous warrior masculinity in the late nineteenth century, Geronimo.

> Step inside the militant minded
> Confined him inside assigned confinement
> Picture the best
> Pac and Nas combined with
> Russell and Dennis at an AIM protest[24]

He connects the past with perhaps two of the most iconic and revered rappers in hip hop history: Tupac Shakur and Nasir Jones. They are known, though, not only for their dope lyrics, but also their ability to be a relevant voice of struggle for the black and oppressed masses. By linking these rappers with Dennis Banks and Russell Means, and, implicitly, the radical history of AIM, he is able to bridge the red power movement, the hip hop generation, and the Indigenous hip hop generation. Indeed, he goes on to rap,

I'm not a rapper

I'm an activist that rhymes

With these two lines, Nataanii Means lucidly places his art within the context of activism, inspired by his father. His role, as an Indigenous warrior living in modernity, is to be a voice of the people, challenging colonialism.

One of the major problems that Native people face are hipsters in headdresses. The video shows a picture of a hipster in a headdress flashing quickly on the left side of the screen at the same time that Means raps the line:

Got a bullet for the next hipster in a headdress

Step aside

I got that C-4 flow

I'm ready to blow at any minute

Motherfucker let me go

In the last part of the video, he shows a short clip of his father describing what the term "radical" means in the context of Native people attempting to end colonialism. Russell Means states,

I wanna talk a little bit about radicalism and being called radical. You know, maybe it is true I am a radical. Because all I've ever asked, all I've ever demanded, all I've ever fought for, all I've ever been shot for, all I've been ever stabbed or beaten for, or thrown in jail or prison for, is to ask and demand, any way, shape or form, that the United States live up to its own laws.[25]

Reeducation of the Red and White Man

You will see the name Frank Waln several times throughout this book. The cat can spit! What makes his work relevant for me is that it is another example of Indigenous modernity. In December 2015, he dropped a new joint that I had to cop; he also got mad love from Indigenous people on social media. The track is called "What Makes the Red Man Red," and it is an example of signifyin'. Signifyin' is one of four modes of black American discourse, including call-response, narrative sequencing, and tonal semantics; these broad discourses also exist in rap music.[26] Signifyin', or signfication, "refers to the verbal art of insult in which a speaker humorously puts down, talks about, needles that is, signifies on the listener. Sometimes signifyin' (also siggin') is done to make a point, sometimes it's just for fun."[27] But signifyin' can also have a direct message, such as Frank's track. It can be a way of "teaching or driving home a cognitive message." Furthermore, signifyin' can have all of these characteristics:

> indirection, circumlocution; metaphorical-imagistic (but images rooted in the everyday, real world); humorous, ironic; rhythmic fluency and sound; teachy but not preachy directed at person or persons usually present in the situational context (siggers do not talk behind yo back); punning, play on words; introduction of the semantically or logically unexpected.[28]

Now, imagine listening to your favorite rap song while applying Smitherman's breakdown of the specific details of this particular form of discourse. I bet you can hear all of these modes of discourse throughout the song. "What Makes the Red Man Red," from its name to the calling out of the contradictions of racism, more than fits the definition of signifyin',

> Your history books (lies)/ Your holidays (lies)
> Thanksgiving lies and Columbus Day
> Tell me why I know more than the teacher
> Tell me why I know more than the preacher
> Tell me why you think the red man is red
> Stained with the blood from the land you bled
> Tell me why you think the red man is dead
> With a fake headdress on your head
> Tell me what you know about thousands of Nations

> Displaced and confined to concentration camps
>
> called reservations
>
> We died for the birth of your nation.[29]

The song itself begins with the infamous (and extremely racist) scene from *Peter Pan* in which Peter and those little rich kids are hanging out with the stoic Indians; they dance, sing, and engage with the dreaded red man. Repeatedly we hear, "What makes the red man red!" If you have not seen this scene, it is, admittedly, very jarring. But Frank's quick, strong voice and lyrics make you forget about that, even as the song plays faintly in the background.

In this first half of the first version, Frank asks important rhetorical questions of the audience, who are presumably settlers and their educational, religious, and social systems. He asks them why he knows more about what it is actually like to be Indigenous than the preacher and teacher do, even though they tell Native people that the way they live their lives is heathen and wrong. Frank is, without a doubt, a master signifier.

> Hollywood portrays us wrong (like savages)
>
> History books say we're gone (like savages)
>
> Your god and church say we're wrong (like savages)
>
> We're from the Earth, it made us strong

He then brilliantly connects the past and the present, from Hollywood's portrayal of Indigenous people, to religion, to textbooks, which, arguably, don't even mention Native people after the Trail of Tears (which represents only *one* Cherokee story!). He then goes on to explain who the real "savage" is in verse two:

> Savages is as savage does
>
> The white man came and ravaged us
>
> Caused genocide / look in my eyes
>
> and tell me who you think the savages was

In the second verse, Frank puts a mirror to settlers, asking them to accept their past and deal with its consequences. Indigenous so-called

savagery is a product of the white imagination as are the violent consequences of it. This is a tricky thing, though. For, as black queer writer
James Baldwin writes, the major problem of white America is that they
"desire not to be judged by those who are not white, not to be seen as
[they] [are], and at the same time a vast amount of the white anguish is
rooted in the white man's equally profaned need to be seen as he is, to be
released from the tyranny of his mirror."[30] In this regard, settlers continue creating the "savage" image with headdresses because they cannot
come to grips with the profound emptiness of what it means to be white
today. To make Frank's point plain and based upon the tone of his voice,
he is straight-up sayin' that it takes a savage to know a "savage" mufucka!
He's a boss for that one! I believe that this strong language and tone is
necessary, at least momentarily, for the liberation of a people who simply
don't exist outside of racist mascots and hipsters rockin' headdresses.

A part of constructing Indigenous modernity is to hold this mirror
up for settlers, to help them see their own lack of humanity. Frank does
this through rapping. What makes the red man red? Settlers' lack of
humanity and their whiteness create a red man, a savage. It allows them
to construct an image that is supposedly less than their own. Frank is able
to undermine settler imaginaries through his lyrics while also uplifting
Indigenous humanity, and, imperatively, Indigenous peoples' ability to
be modern subjects.

Chapter Two

THE FASHION OF INDIGENOUS HIP HOP

Introduction

A dope educator, a white woman I know, asked me to join the #HipHopEd hashtag on Twitter during a cool, fall Tuesday evening in 2015. They do a two-hour conversation every Tuesday, in which people discuss contemporary usage of hip hop in a variety of educational settings, and also reminisce about hip hop back in the day. These conversations cross generations, and are informative and useful for hip hop heads, fans, and educators. Check it out.

Before my first run, I contemplated how I would engage with the vast users of #HipHopEd. These things require strategy. You don't want to be too academic because someone might try and troll you for being too "book smart," but you also don't want to insult the practitioners of a culture I study like a fan-scholar. After all, they are the creators. I searched through to see what cats was tweeting about and then I decided to ask the question that burns my hip hop soul: Why did people in the Soul Sonic Force rock a headdress? I mean, that shit ain't cool. Responses varied, but one of the more interesting ones went something like, "they were paying homage to Native people and the culture." That answer, or rather perspective, don't fly as an excuse. The logic of black Americans wearing chief headdresses and European-created symbols is disappointing, even infuriating. We need to do better in how we relate to each other, *especially* in how we relate to each other.

Fashion has always been a major part of hip hop culture. From the jean jacket vests to Run DMC's track "My Adidas," those in the hip hop game take their clothing seriously. An important work that explores the history of hip hop fashion is Elena Romero's *Freestylin': How Hip Hop*

Changed the Fashion Industry (2012). This book documents the rise of hip hop fashion, and the people who made it happen. The recent documentary *Fresh Dressed*, a film by Sacha Jenkins, illustrates the importance of fashion to hip hop culture. Some of the older generation might hate on the young folks for their love of material goods. However, the love for how one looks or how bad one is on the mic, is arguably an extension of their hip hop godfathers and godmothers. Ain't nuttin wrong with that. Native hip hop artists, too, have their own style. Some are an extension of their particular tribal clans; others rock more challenging forms of Native gear.

In this brief chapter, I argue that Indigenous hip hop fashion is another avenue through which Native artists construct themselves as modern subjects. As Elena Romero contends, hip hop fashion is a way of being. "It is part of the set of norms deriving from hip hop culture, which also has certain ideas, ideals, values, knowledge, and ways of knowing."[1] At the same time, while they are creating their own niche within the larger hip hop community—that is, people *know* they are Native by their gear—others attempt to challenge the settler colonial politics of fashion by reversing the meaning of a racist mascot. Native fashion in hip hop culture is about Native people asserting their own sense of being in hip hop. It is their humanity, expressed through fashion. My objective in this chapter is to very briefly highlight a few hip hop artists who I see engaging in Native fashion in creative ways that both challenge and at other times reproduce ideas of Indigenous authenticity and settler tropes of Native people. But first we must return to hip hop's formative years, where Indigenous representations have existed.

Representations of Indigeneity in Hip Hop Culture

Since hip hop's formation, representations of indigeneity have been a part of the culture. Unfortunately it was rooted in stereotypes. For instance, Pow Wow, a member of The Soul Sonic Force, led by Afrika Bambaataa, wore a headdress on the front of the album cover to their hit single "Planet Rock." This is one of the most influential early hip hop tracks of all time, and people have just skipped over the fact that these black folks were also wearing a headdress (as well as other recent allegations of sexual abuse involving Bambaataa). Beyond hip hop, we see the contradictions of black folks like Pharrell Williams wearing a headdress on the cover of *Elle* magazine in the summer of 2014; also, rapper T.I., from Atlanta, Georgia, uses a chief head as the symbol for his Grand Hustle Gang brand. They may not be malicious in intention, but Indigenous representations of Native people are rooted in noble savagery in hip hop culture. The concept of the "noble savage" goes back to the era of European Enlightenment; it "really pointed to the possibility of progress by civilized man if left free and untrammeled by outworn institutions."[2] In other words, Europeans' perceived idea of the simple Native life served as a "thoroughgoing critique of European social institutions and cultural values."[3] It is difficult to explain the function of Indigenous representations in hip hop culture, but if I could speculate, I would imagine black folks find something noble in Native histories, a white settler masculine version, where they desire to align themselves with being a chief, the best artist in the game. Unfortunately, this still perpetuates European-created images of Native people.

This kind of representation is not so much "playing Indian" in the sense of Phil Deloria; instead, it is a reproduction of black folks reproducing these racist representations, but layered further in the vestiges of blackness. There is no simple answer to explain why black folks desire to engage in performing settler ideas of Indianness, but I suppose we could also ask the same question about why men of color also reproduce gender violence; we live in the twenty-first century, and have long dealt with the effects of colonialism and racism, even if we have a responsibility to break down those forms of violence as best we can.

The point here is that settler colonial representations of Indigenous people and cultures are fundamental to hip hop culture. In this way, Native people are not only reclaiming their space within hip hop culture, but they are also producing new aesthetics that directly confront the colonialism and create new possibilities of representations of Indigenous cultures. What a time to be alive!

Indigenous hip hop fashion, like hip hop fashion in its earlier roots, is about the expression of self and culture. Jessica Metcalfe, founder of "Beyond Buckskin," an online fashion blog and clothing boutique, argues that Native fashion designers and artists make clothing and artifacts more "Indian" by infusing "tribal aesthetic design into fashion, while educating others and allowing patrons to express, define, and perform their varying notions of Indianness."[4] Importantly, as Metcalfe further contends, contemporary Native fashion should not be dismissed as not "traditional." After all, as she points out, "an historical analysis of Indian attire has shown us that Native people have always incorporated new materials and ideas into their preexisting frameworks, even before European contact."[5] Native artists rock Native bling (Native beading) usually with a medallion that represents something about their particular nation or clan, or something that is not Native per se but that represents something they like, which would be akin to wearing a gold chain with a Jesus piece. Of course, they must deal with the caveat of having to create alternative forms of fashion in places and/or spaces where so-called "native" fashion exists everywhere. For instance, the Navajo Nation is suing Urban Outfitters for trademark infringement because the retailer sold "Navajo panties," which is straight disrespectful on so many levels. Indigenous hip hop fashion seems to be in its infancy, but like hip hop fashion in general, hopefully it can gain a wider audience, with the hopes of also creating revenue for artists while also raising awareness about the lunacy of using Indian mascots to represent sports teams. I now turn to several artists who illustrate a variety of perspectives on Indigenous fashion.

Miss Chief Rocka

Miss Chief Rocka, whose name is Angela Miracle Gladue, is an Indigenous b-girl from Edmonton, Alberta, Canada. She created her alter ego in order to represent both her First Nations and hip hop cultural identities. In my understanding of what she means, it is not so much living in two worlds as it is producing an Indigenous identity rooted in hip hop's (also black) cultural modernity. That is, a part of hip hop's modernity allows for her, an Indigenous woman, to represent herself in a way that acknowledges two distinct cultures, which she, like other Indigenous artists, is rapidly blending. She is a Fancy Shawl dancer and a b-girl. For the purposes of this chapter, I want to focus on one component of her work, her bead-work, or what she calls "Native bling."

Beading has long been an Indigenous cultural act of production. It can serve many purposes and illustrate many types of things. For instance, one of my Detroit homies, Lisa Brunk, will bead one's dodem, or clan, on a medallion that can be worn as a part of powwow regalia or for other purposes. Gladue's work is dedicated to her late brother, Anthony Marino Gladue. She writes on her website, "Beading is definitely a gift of healing, and every stitch that goes into my beadwork is a step towards that. I miss you and love you dearly Tony." Two pieces from her beading stick out: the boom box piece and the Cleveland Indian Skull. They are bling. Importantly, "bling" is a hip hop word, meaning jewelry that shines bright, made popular by hip hop mogul Lil Wayne on the track "Bling Bling," which also features B.G. and Juvenile.

Figure 1. The Indian Chief Head. The Hustle Gang Brand Image. https://www.instagram.com/hustlegangbrand

Figure 2. The "Air Drezus" image. It is a silhouette of Drezus with a tomahawk. Courtesy of Drezus. Used with permission.

The boom box piece has the caption "I Can't Live Without My Radio." That is, of course, a reference to hip hop legend turned actor LL Cool J. The boom box pays homage to both his work and the fact that the boom box is a legendary symbol and history representation in hip hop culture. Importantly, it is done through the Indigenous artistic expression of beading. Here, we see the links between two historical blending of cultures, created for a modern Indigenous and non-Indigenous audience. Here is an important point of Indigenous hip hop fashion, especially in how it is produced: it is for the consumption of everyone. European Americans get up in arms about the fact they cannot appropriate other cultures without consequence, and when they get called out for wearing "tribal" patterns by intellectuals like my homie Adrienne Keene, they start trippin'. They should know that Native people have never said to not wear Native gear or fashion. In fact, I don't think I've ever heard that. More than that, historically and today, Native people have always sold their items to Europeans for profit, especially in the late nineteenth and twentieth centuries, when there were less opportunities for other means of survival. Hell, powwows are public and Indigenous vendors sell their shit to make money, and there is nothing wrong with that—keep gettin' dem checks! However, Indigenous people critique businesses that appropriate patterns and items that are supposed to be Native and are produced for mass, usually European American, consumption.

The piece itself is red and black, with the necklace part having chains. It is both an Indigenous aesthetic created for both Native and non-Native people. More than this, it represents Indigenous modernity, through Native bling. Making this particular type of beading suggests that Gladue is interested in pushing the boundaries of what "traditional" means, while also creating new Indigenous aesthetic possibilities for Native people. This is right in line with the production of Indigenous hip hop culture. Gladue has also produced a piece called "Zulu Nation," which pays homage to Bambattaa's group, the Zulu Nation.

The "Cleveland NDN Skull" piece is a play on the professional Major League Baseball team Cleveland Indians mascot "chief wahoo." Many Native people have used counter images as a visual critique of this racist mascot. Here, though, it is represented on bling. This form of critique has the potential to challenge racist mascots, but it still seems narrowly used by Native people and sympathizers. Hopefully this sort of anticolonial critique will become mainstream, but it is still a useful form of challenging colonialism, especially through Native bling.

Chase Manhattan: Reappropriating Chief Heads

Producer and deejay Chase Manhattan's recent album, *Warrior DNA*, is filled with dope beats and clever lyrics. On the track "How I Feel" he says, "replace the crown with a war bonnet/how ya like me now."[6] As mentioned in an earlier chapter, Chase Manhattan presents a useful opportunity to unpack the intersections of blackness and indigeneity. In another way, it is also important to investigate the politics of his use of Indigenous imagery. To be clear, Manhattan is both challenging colonial imagery while also profiting from it. While we cannot know the impact it might have in changing the visual narrative that racist Indigenous mascots produce, it is important to engage in the art of speculation to see what we might uncover.

Figure 3. Picture of Sicangu Lakota rapper Frank Waln.
Courtesy of Frank Waln. Used with permission.

Chase Manhattan sells a variety of clothing items on his website, including hoodies, snapbacks, tee shirts, and beanies. He makes sure to place on his website his hashtags #FollowMyTribe and #MrHustleTribe. His cultural movement is based on individual expression and hustling by any means necessary. His unique approach to fashion is to make already existing emblems and symbols "indigenous" by placing a feather or tepee on the design. For instance, one way in which he changes already existing symbols is by altering National Football League team mascots to make them more "indigenous."

We can see in this photo that he uses the symbol of the Minnesota Vikings mascot and places a war bonnet on it. The obvious reason for altering is so he does not violate copyright. However, he is also illustrating the importance of his brand to his audience. Though this image has the consequence of challenging colonialism, we do have to question its effectiveness, as it is embedded in the contradictions of Indigenous modernity. On the one hand, through his art he is able to present contemporary representations of a Native-inspired fashion, but he utilizes Plains Indian imagery. In other words, does this actually serve as a form of protest? Or should he be obliged as a Native artist—given the context of how pervasive racist mascots are in the United States—to create protest art? I tend to side with the belief that artists should have freedom of expression in their craft, for art can be polarizing. Regardless, he has a unique opportunity to find creative ways to alter colonial imagery for the point of Indigenous youth social uplift. Still, Chase Manhattan along with other Native artists exist within a web of colonial constructs in which, even as they attempt to carve out a creative Indigenous niche, they are often bound by the limits of colonial imaginings. This invisibility is perhaps unique in how it affects Native people, who are thus bound by its limits.

Chase Manhattan also produces a hyper-Indigenous-masculine version of fashion. The use of the chief imagery is about reinserting contemporary expressions of Indigenous masculinity. Contemporary representations of Indigenous masculinity and Native peoples' attempt to rid themselves of it—like Indigenous people as a whole—remain rooted in colonial notions of it. Like others, Native hip hop artists are

Figure 4. Photo of Sagamok First Nations rapper SouFy from Detroit. Courtesy of SouFy. Used with permission.

attempting to break down those colonial images that still exist in settler states. Manhattan, then, is also a part of that process. In his quest to solidify his name within hip hop culture, he is also trying to reclaim the notion of a chief.

Another artist who attempts to reclaim ideas of "warriorness" is Drezus, who was discussed in chapter one. The "Air Drezus" photo plays on the iconic "Air Jordan" symbol that is used to represent the Michael Jordan shoe brand. Drezus's photo is a representation of masculinity rooted in the stereotypical image of the Indigenous American warrior. He is also holding the gunstock war club, a weapon used by a variety of nations beginning in the seventeenth century. The image Drezus uses is a red silhouette of his body. He holds the war club high above his head, as if signaling to the audience that he is ready for battle. In the background of the silhouette are the words "Drezus Music" in white letters, with the others in the background being in black.[7]

This image signifies a certain type of masculinity. He is, on the one hand, trying to resurrect an idea of masculinity rooted in past exploits of bravery and war. On the other hand, we should question the usefulness of these images, and how they might benefit Native young men, including those who are Two-Spirit or transgender folks. How can we create an Indigenous masculine aesthetic that is inclusive, and at times, less reliant on what an Indigenous warrior is supposed to be? This is something that Indigenous communities must confront going forward.

There are Native artists who represent their Indianness by wearing their hair long, in braids. Artists like Frank Waln adorn themselves with Native bling and rock their hair long. Wearing their hair in braids is important, as it is not something that is supposed to happen in general, and to have younger Native people, especially young Native men see that onstage, is a powerful aesthetic.

Southwest Detroit Anishinaabe rapper SouFy argues that in addition to making his music relevant to contemporary struggles for social justice, the Indigenous hip hop aesthetic is equally important. As he says, "I just know that, when I'm on the microphone or when I'm performing, and when they see you with your hair braided, you're doing something huge."[8] It is not simply that they see his hair, but that they

Figure 5. Picture of rapper and tattoo artist Sten Joddi, founder of Tattoo Muzik Group. Courtesy of Sten Joddi. Used with permission.

have an accurate representation of themselves in popular culture, even hip hop. SouFy even connects language usage and braids as an aesthetic: "Maybe when somebody sees a video or hears the language, they're gonna wanna go learn the language; they might want to get their hair braided because they're favorite rappers' hair is long."[9] Combining the tradition of wearing long braids and adorning the ears with bling, with the performing of hip hop is a remixing of Indigenous aesthetic culture. It is precisely the reason why Native hip hop helps us understand more than just one part of contemporary Indigenous identity construction where people employ and deploy a variety of Indigenous aesthetics and identities, while deftly moving away from a stereotypical one. It also serves as a model for youth as they imagine alternative futures of what an Indigenous cultural identity can look like.

"The Skin We Ink": Tattoos as Indigenous Hip Hop Aesthetic

Hip hop artists adorning their bodies with tattoos, each embedded with their own specific meanings, is a form of cultural literacy embedded with a variety of cultural and social implications for Indigenous expression of self. Writing on the meaning and uses of tattoos as a form of literate expression for young black men, which goes unacknowledged by the standards set in urban education, scholar David E. Kirkland argues that "the body, therefore, has been an important location for understanding the self in the human story of literacy because spilled through the body, the self may render meanings of its own."[10] A similar thing can be said for Indigenous hip hop artists, who, from the unique perspective of Native people, adorn their bodies with tattoos in order to express their humanity as modern subjects. From inking their bodies with feathers to other forms of bodily expression, some artists ink their life story on their bodies as a reminder of where they have come from and where they want to go.

Sten Joddi, a Mvskogee Creek artist, has a label called Tattoo Muzik Group. In the official music video for his track "Faded," Joddi proclaims, "A life full of hieroglyphs/it's written in my skin." Joddi's entire body is covered with tattoos. He has an eagle feather adorned on the left side of his face that goes from the back of his neck to the middle of his cheek, symbolizing how it would appear if he had a real feather brushing against his face in the wind. There are many implications of this. Historically and today, one gets an eagle feather for showing some form of bravery or accomplishing great things in service of your people; it's a sacred thing. As a side note for all of those who like to wear fake headdresses at Coachella and elsewhere: getting an eagle feather is sacred. To make a mockery of it is not only disrespectful but flat-out inhumane. But I digress. Throughout the "Faded" video, the majority of the males show off their tattoos, pointing to them as the camera approaches. Many people are also wearing the Tattoo Muzik Group white tee shirt with black letters.

At about three minutes into the video Joddi has his entire shirt off, and is seen holding a cup of alcohol in his left hand and a microphone in his right. Throughout the video, he also wears a black and white chief head medallion.

On his website, there are images of his face on a tee shirt and the Tattoo Muzik Group emblem. Joddi is also a tattoo artist. According

Figure 6. Miss Chief Rocka rockin the Native bling boombox. Photo Courtesy of Angela Gladue. Photo credit Brad Crowfoot. Used with permission.

to his website, he has been doing tattoos since he was twelve, creating one himself on his arm. For more than eleven years, he has been doing professional tattooing, using the money to "fund his TattooMuzik and Family Life." For Joddi, tattoos are not just the scribbles of his life, they are also a means of support so he can continue doing the other thing he loves: hip hop music.

Tattoo Muzik Group is also about Indigenous entrepreneurship. In order to make a living, Indigenous hip hop artists engage in a variety of activities to support themselves and their families. In their endeavor to carve out a space for themselves in hip hop, they might mentor youth to become mini moguls who not only benefit themselves but also their communities, Indigenous and non-Indigenous, however they see fit.

Photography: Ernie Paniccioli

No one has captured the visuals of hip hop more than Ernie Paniccioli. He is a hip hop legend. He is not a rapper, a deejay, a b-boy, or a graffiti artist; he is almost single-handedly responsible for photographs of hip hop for the last thirty years. Check out some of the artists he has taken photos of: Public Enemy, the Notorious BIG, Lil Lim, Queen Latifah, Run DMC, LL Cool J, Kris Kross, and Lauryn Hill, to name a few. He has also taken photos of graffiti; he's captured the essence of hip hop culture since the beginning. He has also published numerous photographic books, most notably *Who Shot Ya?: Three Decades of Hip Hop Photography* (2002), with Kevin Powell.[11] One of the things known about Paniccioli is that he is Cree.

Ernie Paniccioli was born on February 26, 1947, in the Bedford-Stuyvesant section of Brooklyn. His mother primarily raised him. According to Paniccioli, he grew up "dirt poor." He lived in substandard housing, and his mother often had to choose between paying rent and buying groceries. Though growing up poor, his mother taught him that in order to succeed, one had to read books, which he did often. He also frequented the Brooklyn Museum and the Brooklyn Public Library, which helped foster his love for photography. He also grew up experiencing discrimination.[12]

He recalls that when he was around seven years old, Irish and Italian kids would call him a "little spic," and although he didn't know what it meant, "he didn't like being called it." They would also call him "half-breed," "Pocahontas," and "Little Geronimo." As a result, he would fight—often. He notes that the black kids in his neighborhood would never diss him, though. In fact, while the other kids in the neighborhood messed with him, "the brothers just looked at me and didn't really care; every time they saw me get into a fight they were there on my side. At the age of nine, he joined the Bishops, a black gang.

Paniccioli is as respected an icon in the hip hop game as you will find. Cornell University holds his vast photographic archive. Although those familiar with hip hop know his story, it is important to highlight it in this book because his story is different—it is different because he was an Indigenous person who grew up in the city, and was not bound by the ideas of "authenticity" that vex so many young Indigenous people. While he might not read as "traditional," it is important that he is a Native person who has impacted the visual representations of hip hop since the beginning, and is arguably just as important as the fashion industry associated with hip hop's style. Thus we can argue by extension that indigeneity and hip hop have been intimately linked from the beginning. He helped bind the urban experience of black youth, through the photographic genius of a Cree man, influenced by his mother, Cree, and black culture. His photographs represent Indigenous modernity because his experience serves as a prelude to that of the Indigenous hip hop generation today: influenced by black culture but also, still, Indigenous.

Paniccioli's photographs and place in hip hop should force us to ask a few questions: Must an Indigenous person produce Indigenous-themed art in order for it to be Indigenous? If they do, what does Indigenous-themed art look like? Also, although Paniccioli has consistently acknowledged his Cree identity, it does not seem a salient part of hip hop's early years. Why is that? I don't have an answer to that direct question, but it is important to put it out there for some to ponder. But I do want to engage with the former two.

The question of whether someone is doing Indigenous-themed art is the question that those who consider themselves "traditional" ask when they question Native hip hop artists as to why they are doing the "black thing." To produce Indigenous-themed art, oftentimes, creates a bind for some. On the one hand, it may be someone's unique experience as a Native person, which they illustrate in their art. On the other hand, it might also feed into settler fantasies about "authentic" Indigenous representations. Unfortunately, given European peoples' representations of Native people, this is the conundrum that all Native artists, in any art form, have to deal with. Paniccioli's story and his work suggest that we should unpack and then expand our collective understanding of Indigenous identity, especially as it relates to hip hop. The particularities of his upbringing in an urban environment allow for us to think further about Indigenous identity construction in postwar America. More than this, they afford us an opportunity to think about the many meanings of indigeneity in the formative years of hip hop culture. In other words, from the beginning, indigeneity was a part of the construction of hip hop culture, and it is time we reclaim that.

Asserting/justifying the idea that hip hop was not only a black (and Latinx) cultural construction but also an Indigenous one from the beginning, requires both some creative thinking and explanation. Check it: when a photographer takes a photo, they are constructing the photo. They are paying attention to lighting, the background, the angles at which the photo is taken, instructing the subject in the photo to sit a certain way. In fact, they dictate how the photo will look. It is perhaps only after several photos are snapped that the subject in the photo will have much agency to choose which one will be presented to the public (along with publicists and others).

Paniccioli created an Indigenous aesthetic that is not easily read as Indigenous because it does not fit into settler fantasies of "authentic Native" art, nor does it fit into certain expectations of "Indigenous"-themed art by some of our community members. This Indigenous aesthetic is urban, it is hip hop, and it has black folks in it. He documented a culture that was a part of his cultural upbringing as an Indigenous male in

Brooklyn. Several publics—black, white, and even Indigenous—were able to witness it.

Conclusion

Indigenous hip hop artists have a unique opportunity to create alternative forms of being Indigenous through their fashion. In this way, they can help Native youth see different aesthetics that are not bound by the settler colonial imaginings created by Europeans. At the same time, they have to deal directly with the contradictions embedded in societies that would rather see them maintain invisibility. More than this, Native artists will have to engage with the age-old questions: What is Indigenous hip hop, specifically, and what is Indigenous art more generally? What happens when it does not fit into the standards set by both Indigenous and non-Indigenous societies? What are the boundaries, and where should we place limits on what is and is not Indigenous art? I think the artists should get together and discuss these issues, not to create narrow ideas of what Indigenous art is or is not, but to determine what they should not tolerate insofar as it is not desirable to perpetuate negative images of Native people.

Chapter Three

INDIGENOUS MASCULINITY IN HIP HOP CULTURE

Or, How Indigenous Feminism Can Reform Indigenous Manhood

I came to what we call "Indigenous feminism" through stories about my great-grandmother, Esther Shawboose Mays. Her contemporaries described her as a "fiery" woman, a person who did not take shit from nobody! For some reason, I have always relished that narrative. When I say that I learned Indigenous feminism through stories about my great-grandmother, I mean it. Let me be clear: I do not call myself a feminist, even while attempting every day to check my male patriarchy and support my sister/as. I do not have a problem with men who call themselves feminists; I just think it is better to move in silence. (At the same time, of course, I believe in speaking up when necessary and/or when asked, but most especially behind closed doors, when you can confront sexism with a homie. The personal is political, too!) For me, while there is burgeoning work in the field of Indigenous feminism, I use the story of my great-grandmother and her children to construct the narrative.

My great-grandmother died of heart failure in June 1984. I was born in 1987. Yet, while being with family in Detroit, on the Saginaw Chippewa Reservation, I would hear stories about her. Her children adored her. She helped found Detroit's Indian Educational and Cultural Center (DIECC). My aunt Judy Mays, her daughter, was the DIECC's first educational coordinator and, later, the founder and first principal of the third-ever US public school with a Native American curriculum: Medicine Bear American Indian Academy. I learned about their exploits in the Motor City back in the day, and gained a deeper appreciation for the work of Native women. Then, I studied it. Women like Esther Shawboose Mays and Judy Mays taught several generations of youth how to care about the community, and to be active in it. They carried civilization, but in a broad, modern sense. They understood that in postwar Detroit, there were a variety of ways of being Indigenous in the world, and to limit it to those who were "full-blooded" or only Anishinaabe, would cause great detriment to their community. Their activism, through cultural revitalization and education, was the root of their feminism. Moreover, specific to them, they are a part of the Makwa dodem (bear clan). A part of their cultural responsibilities is to be a protector and healer of their clan, community, and nation.

What I have learned, and what Indigenous men myself included should strive for, is to continue to learn from our grandmothers, aunts, cousins, sisters, nieces, and non–gender binary people in our families and communities in order to resurrect our masculinities. Indigenous feminism is not tied to gendered bodies; rather, it is a perspective that cares for our community, as well as our non-Indigenous relatives.

Indigenous masculinity cannot be one in which we use rhetoric such as "taking care of our women" or framing women in a way that primarily upholds patriarchy. While we all suffer under the cloak of colonialism, that does not mean that everyone in our communities experiences it the same. We have a role and a responsibility to ourselves and to our communities to challenge patriarchy, and to teach the next generation to be more progressive and loving in our social relations. Indeed, if Indigenous masculinity is going to be anything worthwhile in the twenty-first century, then it needs to be rooted in care for community and love of humanity.

Indigenous feminism, as a field of academic inquiry, has been around for a long time, though I begin with Patricia Albers and Beatrice Medicine's important work, *The Hidden Half* (1983). Since then, numerous Native women have clearly defined the terms of Indigenous feminism in at least two ways. While there are variances, I see contemporary Indigenous feminist scholarship in two camps. First, there are those who define it in limited, nationalistic terms. I still consider Laura Tohoe's piece to be the defining one, in which she declared, "There is no word for feminism in my language."[1] There is also the camp that tends to view Indigenous feminism in ways that advocate for defining it in progressive, nonbinary terms. Though rooted in particular Indigenous communities' cultural milieus, they can still take from and utilize contemporary realities to define feminism. Again, while I do not define myself as a feminist, I fall into the latter camp because it leaves open possibilities of what it has, can, and might mean to be an Indigenous feminist. My version of feminism is informed by the work of Maile Arvin, Eve Tuck, and Angie Morrill. In their article "Decolonizing Feminism: Challenging Connection between Settler Colonialism and Heteropatriarchy" (2013), they outline what they call "Native feminist theories" to address the disconnect between mainstream feminism found in gender and women's studies and ethnic studies, and their inability to deal with settler colonialism. They write,

> We define Native feminist theories as those theories that make sub-stantial advances in understandings of the connections between settler colonialism and both heteropatriarchy and heteropaternalism. Native feminist theories focus compound issues of gender, sexuality, race, indigeneity, and nation.[2]

Settler colonialism is key to understanding any Indigenous feminist theory, and Indigenous people at large. They continue, "[W]ithin the context of land and settler colonialism, the issues facing Indigenous women, as inseparable from the issues facing Indigenous peoples as a whole, are resolved via decolonization and sovereignty, not (just parity)."[3]

I define Indigenous feminism as a way of being Indigenous and feminine (I mean this in multiple ways) in the modern world. Indigenous feminism is not bound by ideas of "authenticity" or "tradition"; nor is it bound to gendered bodies. It is an approach, a way of viewing the world, something we can learn through the organizing efforts of Indigenous women, trans people, and people of all genders. It is based upon how Native women actually live(d) their lives, and what they project to the world. One can embody it; one can perform it. Above all, it is rooted in the specifics of place, that is, where one grows up and where one calls home.

While we might be inclined to define Indigenous feminism in ways that are particular to one's tribal nation, women like Esther and Judy (and her siblings) grew up in black Detroit. Judy and her siblings had a black father. They lived in the heart of black cultural production. They enjoyed the soul and sounds of Motown; the joys of gathering with Native people and hearing the heartbeat of the people—the drum—at local powwows. Did this make them less Indigenous than others? No. They were Saginaw Chippewa, but they did not live in a vacuum. Their Indigenous feminism was influenced by the work of DRUM (Dodge Revolutionary Union Movement), with whom my Aunt Judy participated with briefly.[4]

In fact, we should be open to acknowledging that Native feminism can learn from and even take from women of color feminisms. As Renya Ramirez reminds us, "We should be open to reading the writings of women of color feminists in order to help [us] theorize Native feminist theory and praxis."[5] Most importantly, Indigenous feminism is about fighting not only for the rights of Native women but for the whole community and nation. I do not mean this in the sense of women being the "creators" of civilizations and nations while they carry children, there are multiple types of families and ways to care for children. Framing the role of women in this way also limits their possibility and potentials for continuing to better our communities.

Gender in Hip Hop Studies

The study of gender in hip hop studies has exploded in the last several years. From Tricia Rose's poignant articulation of the "commercial hip-hop trinity"—gangsta, pimp, and ho—to the recently published edited collection by Ruth Nicole Brown and Chamara Kwakye (2012), gender (and sexuality) has emerged as a salient feature for understanding the complexities of bodies—especially black (female) bodies—in hip hop.[6] Also, the work of scholarship in hip hop feminism has allowed for us to better understand the experiences of black women in hip hop culture, moving them from the margins to centering their experiences.[7] Even filmmakers have explored the construction of hypermasculinity in hip hop.[8] While these works are important, they have tended to focus solely (for good reason) on regressive elements of (black) masculinity.

Beyond hip hop studies, scholars have focused on black masculinity from multiple angles. For example, scholars such as Victor Rios have shown how urban environments have used a "youth control complex" to police the lives of black (and Latinx) bodies.[9] He convincingly shows how our most vulnerable young men begin to internalize this constant (racial) policing. By the time they reach adolescence, the only manhood they have developed is one that is related to being tough. This toughness stems from police surveillance, gang activity, and going in and out of correctional facilities. By then, it is often too late; they no longer have the ability to form alternative forms of masculinity.

Other scholars have explored this process of internalization in popular culture, in particular the relationship between death and black masculinity. Cultural studies scholar Aimé Ellis has argued that contemporary young black men are "lured by both the finality that death ostensibly assures and the virulent masculinity that deathly violence and death-defiance work to produce."[10] Yet in this contemporary moment, black men have a difficult time constructing alternative forms of masculinity particularly during a time when one in three are basically summoned to a social or physical death during the era of the "New Jim Crow."[11] Indeed, as Ellis argues, "deathly violence and death-defiance manifest as a desperate attempt for black men to both assert their manhood and preserve their humanity by resisting domination and retaining separateness."[12]

In addition to Rios, bell hooks has written extensively about black manhood. At the core of black masculinity is an attempt at the destruction of black men in general. "At the center of the way black male selfhood is constructed in white-supremacist capitalist patriarchy," writes hooks, "is the image of the brute—untamed, uncivilized, unthinking, and unfeeling."[13] Framing black masculinity in this way, which I believe to be true, is also a way to kill, literally, black men. The same logic exists in Amerikkka: an attempt to kill black men. Native men suffer under a similar aim, to kill them, albeit in a different method.

Indigenous masculinity is rooted in a culture where they no longer exist. A key feature of Indigenous dispossession is to make them invisible with the aim of gaining land. Of course this process goes beyond

Indigenous men, it also impacts Indigenous social relations at large, but the way that settler society constructs Indigenous masculinity today is largely seen through warriors of the past. Indeed, we can look at the use of Indigenous mascots, including that sports team in Washington, D.C., and the nostalgic way in which people hold on to something that is of their imagination. The list can go on in college and professional sports: the Chicago Blackhawks, the Cleveland Indians, the Atlanta Braves, the Florida State Seminoles, and countless high school teams throughout the country.

All of these settler symbols have a few things in common: first is an implicit statement about the conquering of Indigenous people, including Indigenous manhood and land (the two are connected). Indeed, to dispossess Indigenous people is literally and metaphorically the dispossession of men from the source of life, the women, Mother Earth—the mother of us all. Second, these settler symbols are also an explicit celebration of the crisis of white masculinity, historically and today. In order to construct themselves as the epitome of modernity and civilization, white men use Indigenous images to make meaning of their own racialized masculinity.[14] In spite of the attempts at ruining Indigenous manhood, there is hope, and Indigenous hip hop artists present an interesting case to analyze its current manifestations.

In this chapter I examine how Indigenous feminism can contribute to the restoration of Indigenous masculinity, through hip hop culture. I analyze a variety of artists, including Frank Waln, as an example of masculinity that is progressive and, therefore, an example for young Native men. I also want to acknowledge that not everything in Native communities is perfect, and we should not ignore that. In addition to highlighting the very positive and informative parts of Indigenous masculinity, I also want to highlight the less progressive versions of Indigenous masculinity, including some of the misogyny in hip hop music. The blatant version of masculinity is easy to uncover; what is difficult is the subtler version from those who would consider themselves "nationalists." That perspective is not useful for the future of Native communities, either.

There is a lot that Native hip hop can add to the conversation and (re)construction of Indigenous masculinity today. A key part of reconstructing Indigenous masculinity is to avoid the insulting and patriarchal notion of "protecting" our women. As Glen Coulthard notes, this perspective only "serves to reinforce the symbolic violence of assuming that Indigenous women are ours to protect."[15]

Indigenous Hip Hop as Indigenous Masculinity

Perhaps a major point of contention is the belief that Native rappers are trying to act black. Read another way—in a deep-structure kind of way—this is someone telling Native rappers that they are trying to perform and mimic a form of black masculinity that is exuded through hip hop culture. There is a great deal of scholarship on black masculinity.[16] These scholars have analyzed black masculinity as a form of literacy and as a part of black popular culture. I want to use a definition of (black) hip hop masculinity provided by Timothy J. Brown. He writes that a "hip-hop black masculinity is a site of struggle displaying both progressive and regressive constructions of masculinity."[17] It is the intersection of progressive and regressive that I want to unpack.

Hip hop has its raw energy, language, misogyny, disrespect of women (and I mean women of color) and members of the LBGTQ+2 community, but it is a product of society. If hip hop died tomorrow, these social ills would still vex our society. The same could be said of how Indigenous masculinity is represented in hip hop culture; that is, the performance of colonialism—homophobia and sexism within hip hop culture, for instance—is also a product of society, or settler colonialism. However, there is very little scholarship on Native men in contemporary times.[18] Yet, there is one recent edited collection that—literally—gets the conversation going. In the collection, *Masculindians: Conversations About Indigenous Manhood* (2015), author Sam McKegney interviews twenty-three Indigenous people in Canada. They vary from geographic location and Indigenous connection, and include men, women, and Two-Spirit people. Through these interviews, McKegney pushes us to consider the many ways that Indigenous manhood is being defined today. Though the Indigenous artists therein offer more precise discussions of Indigenous masculinity (and often related to their particular community), McKegney has his own useful contribution to make to the conversations.

He writes that masculinity can be "a tool for describing the qualities, actions, characteristics, and behaviours that accrue meaning within a given historical context and social milieu through their association with maleness, as normalized, idealized, and even demonized within a web of power-laden interpenetrating discourses."[19] Though I agree, I also tend to think of Indigenous masculinity in general as a site of potential. I see it as a way of being male (not subscribing to the strict biological definitions of it) in the world, defined through (but not solely by) colonialism, racism, settler imaginings, and, of course, their own construction (or agency) of it.

For my purposes, Indigenous men define their masculinity through hip hop culture. In addition, because Native male rappers are defining and constructing masculinity through hip hop culture a black cultural form they are consequently interacting and engaging with a form of black masculinity in both progressive and regressive forms. Importantly, this allows us to get beyond discussing Indigenous masculinity through the Indigenous-settler binary, which is something that *Masculindians* fails to do. This begs the question: In what ways can we discuss modern Indigenous popular cultures that are not solely defined by their resistance or engagement with colonialism? This is something to think about. To be clear, I am not suggesting that we simply disregard colonialism as a category; however, there are more components within what we might call a settler regime that exist and that need to be discussed. I frame my understanding of an Indigenous hip hop masculinity in at least three categories, all centered on the warrior masculinity: the regressive warrior, the progressive warrior, and the nineteenth-century warrior 2.0. Check it.

Regressive warrior. These are those who quite simply reproduce the misogyny that we see in mainstream hip hop. These artists rap mainly about making money, flashing their Native bling, and conquering Native women's bodies. At the same time, while we can think of Native rappers in this category (and the others), they often present more socially conscious lyrics and often work in Native communities trying to uplift youth, and that should not go unacknowledged.

Progressive warrior. These are those who, to the best of their ability, fight for their communities and attempt to have some engagement with them, including Native women and others within their analysis. They question the imposition of patriarchy and the relegation of Native women into the backdrop of social change.

The nineteenth-century warrior 2.0. These are those artists (and it's not just limited to hip hop) who utilize historical images of warriors from the past, like Geronimo and Crazy Horse, to construct their hip hop masculinity today. It is not that this is necessarily negative, but one has to wonder how productive it is, especially if they do not include multiple forms of masculine performances within their artistic expression.

In the quest for Indigenous sovereignty, Native rappers, especially men, can help move us toward a progressive version masculinity. "Men" are not the only people that can contribute to the reconstruction of Indigenous masculinity. Women and non–gender conforming persons have a great deal to contribute to masculinities in Indigenous communities. I think Native hip hop artists are constructing a warrior masculinity for the twenty-first century. They are "warriors without weapons."

This masculinity is historically rooted but articulated and designed for today's Indigenous people. I think the best ones are actively trying to construct this masculinity from their communities, including from women. One way in which Native men construct masculinity is, again, through settler and historically constructed images. They use these images to their own benefit in order to inspire their communities to rise up against colonialism. They rely on these historical images to create a new reality of and for Indigenous men, through hip hop.

However, that should also raise a red flag. In other words, I am compelled to ask a virtually unanswerable and immeasurable question: How *much* can these artists reappropriate these images and histories for their own benefit? It is difficult to tell. For example, anthropologist Maureen Schwarz writes wonderfully about how Native people since the 1960s have used settler-created images for their own benefit, stating, "rather than protesting [these images], they are currently earmarking images from it and using them for their own ends."[20] Schwarz sees Native people using a variety images to challenge colonialism. On the one hand, Schwarz is obviously correct; Native people have always adapted and manipulated conditions in both the cultural and political spheres as best they could. Indeed, we might even call this the essence of Indigenous modernity. So on one hand they do have agency to challenge colonialism, yet on the other they can also willfully choose to *not* challenge it. It is not my intention to throw my Indigenous sistas and brothas under the bus, but I am not saying anything controversial. If we are actually serious about decolonization, we need to deal with things both how they actually exist and how we want to imagine them to be. However, Indigenous women in our communities have inspired and helped shape the reimagining of Indigenous masculinity for some.

Frank Waln and "My Stone": How Native Women Helped Raise a Lakota Man

I first met Frank Waln in October 2015. We did some work together in Madison, Wisconsin, which I will explain in a later chapter. I first came to know about him when one of my homies told me about this song ("My Stone") from a "Lakota dude" named Frank Waln. As an Anishinaabe, you always get skeptical when you hear of a Lakota—some historical beef still in my blood I suppose (I'm joking). As I listened to the track I began to tear up. Damn, I thought, he put so much of his heart in the lyrics. I read "My Stone" as an anthem, a call for Native men to restore themselves (their masculinity) by acknowledging the beauty and strength that we can learn from our mothers. Frank is the product of an abusive relationship, and his mother raised him alone. Yet, he celebrates his mother, and her ability to make him into the man he is today.

One of my fondest memories of Frank is during a performance before performing "My Stone." Frank restated what the women in his family have always told him: "You don't need to be related to a woman to see her as a human being." That is quite a profound statement. The profoundness is in its simplicity. Yes, perhaps it seems obvious to women. But

I wonder, as I am sure others do, how can a man who claims to love his mother also degrade women? We can see this in hip hop: How can a man who purports to love women, still dehumanize women? Just to be clear: I am not blaming hip hop for the social ills of this society. Regardless, Frank Waln's "My Stone" is an example of what womanhood can teach and also how it can shape Indigenous manhood, in very material ways.

The importance of this song is that it is based upon a Lakota origins story. Waln skillfully places it within the context of his mother being a stone, the strength of his own masculinity. Too often, we place emphasis on the need for a male figure in the construction of masculinity. "My Stone" presents for us an alternative reality, or at least opens up the possibility that Indigenous masculinity can be restored through the efforts and stories of our mothers and great-grandmothers. In the chorus, Frank states,

> Lived all my life
> Just me and you
> Times got tough and you seen me through
> I ain't have a dad
> We ain't have a plan
> Raised by a woman who made me a man.[21]

In reimagining Native masculinity, we must realize that we do not need to rely on the Western idea of heterosexual social relations. In fact, we should embrace all types of families, however it becomes necessary to raise an Indigenous child in the modern world, where they can be Indigenous and healthy. Above all, Indigenous young men need to know that they can love themselves, their communities, and their people, while performing progressive forms of masculinity that uplift their communities.

Frank Waln's "My Stone" reminds me of Tupac Shakur's "Dear Mama." And do not forget: Tupac's "Dear Mama" was inducted into the Library of Congress' National Recording Registry.[22] Check it: His mother is his stone. He was raised by a single mother, unfortunately an all-too-familiar story of a single mother raising a child, a son. A deeper reading of this song, though, offers a potential for articulating the source of Indigenous peoples', especially men's, strength: Indigenous women.

The scholarship on Indigenous women is insightful but limited only limited in the sense that, while we have yet to fully rediscover the important role of Native women in history and society, they have always been the backbone of our communities. I do not mean it in the patriarchal sense of, they produced children and therefore the nation; I mean it to suggest that they have long struggled on the front lines of challenging colonialism, racism, and also sexism inside and outside of our communities. As a result, Indigenous feminism, or the work of Native women as teachers, activists, mothers, scholars, and as Indigenous people, can teach us a lot about not only Indigenous women's place in our community, but also help restore a missing part of many Native communities: Indigenous masculinity.

Indigenous hip hop artists present a variety of forms of Indigenous masculinity. I believe that is where we might want to look for the next generation as a source of potential with caution for restoring Indigenous manhood. By no means do I think this is the perfect or *only* way. As I have shown, I still believe there is much to learn from Indigenous women and non–gender binary people in our communities about what it means to be a "man." We should also utilize our historical knowledge to help resurrect it. We should not, however, use so-called "traditions" as the only mechanism through which we reconstruct Indigenous manhood. That would be a tragedy and serve to perpetuate stereotypes about Indigenous manhood.

Importantly, asserting alternative forms of masculinity will require that we admit and even embrace our vulnerabilities as Indigenous men. This will not be easy. As Leanne Simpson writes in *Decolonial Love,*

> We're all hunting around for acceptance, intimacy, connection and love, but we don't know what those particular medicines even look like so we're just hunting away with vague ideas from dreams and hope and intention, at the same time dragging around blockades full of reminders that being vulnerable has never ended well for any of us, not even one single time.[23]

In our hunt to end settler patriarchy, we must acknowledge that many times being vulnerable has not always worked well for us. And yet, we must continue to strive to change. We must recall that Indigenous manhood today is a product of settler colonialism. Even though Indigenous men have a lot to work on to better themselves, it cannot be divorced from that context. Period. As Robert Innes states, "For Indigenous men, the assimilation process meant . . . that Indigenous ideals of masculinity had to be replaced to conform to a masculinity that upheld the White supremacist heteronormative patriarchy."[24]

I write from a perspective of love. We need to relearn how to love each other and express it, hell, even say it to one another. But we, too, need protection, of our emotions. Author and activist bell hooks provides some useful insight into how we might begin to process this, "until we begin collectively to protect the emotional life of black boys and men we sign their death warrants."[25] This seems true, we must work together everyone in our communities must work to protect the emotional and mental lives of Indigenous men (and others, too). As hooks continues, "Saving the lives of black boys and men requires of us all the courage to challenge patriarchal manhood, the courage to put in its place alternative visions of healing black masculinity."[26] We have a lot of work to do, but in order to perform and live a progressive form of masculinity, we must do it by healing ourselves, through a sovereignty of love. After all, what is the point of sovereignty if we do not love one another? In our quest for a decolonial manhood, we should rely on the love and example of the women in our communities, both past and present, for were it not for their efforts and work to end colonialism, we would not be here today.

Eekwol: Toward an Indigenous Hip Hop Feminist Framework

Eekwol is perhaps one of the old school, OG (original gangsta) Indigenous hip hop feminists, along with Kinnie Starr. Eekwol, a Cree rapper, has been in the game for a minute, and is definitely a cultural theorist of Indigenous feminism. Responding to how men react to her with back-handed compliments such as, "You're good, for a woman," Eekwol lets them cats know that she is just a rapper. In an interview she did in 2008 and responding to a comment about her experience as an Indigenous woman in hip hop, she states, "I'm a rapper first and foremost. And then

I'm a woman. I'm Indigenous, but I'm a rapper; that's my art, that's my creative outlet."[27] I understand this to mean that while she is all three, in the hip hop game she wants to be respected as a bad-ass Indigenous rapper. For me, she is an Indigenous hip hop feminist, which I will explain below. First, though, I want to draw the reader's attention to the work of Aisha Durham, a black hip hop feminist. She defines hip hop feminism as,

> . . . a sociocultural, intellectual, and political movement grounded in the situated knowledge of women of color from the broader hip hop or the U.S. post-civil rights generation who recognize culture as a pivotal site for political intervention to challenge, resist, and mobilize collectives to dismantle systems of exploitation.[28]

This definition offers a healthy combination of women's agency, and their ability to respond to sexism and racism through a culture. While Durham offers an important definition that we can draw from and argues that it can be applied to women of color, she leaves out Indigenous women (surely by omission), for if she included them, settler colonialism and subsequently decolonization would show up in her book, which it does not. I know that was not her subject matter, but all too often, women's and gender studies and hip hop studies exclude settler colonialism as a category of analysis.[29]

Still, I find Durham's definition useful because it provides us with an opportunity to start the process of creating and imagining an Indigenous hip hop feminist framework. I use the word "framework" to suggest that it allows for a fluidity of Indigenous women's experiences to be expressed within the context of a settler colonial society. For one, an Indigenous hip hop feminist framework is not bound by the colonial ideas of who is and who is not Indigenous in the sense of blood quantum and colonial ideas of recognition. Nor is it bound to those who live on or off of the reserve/ation. This framework centers on colonialism but is in a constant state of reaction to it, constantly challenging it and dealing with the outcome of colonialism. It is fundamentally about decolonization. Importantly, the biological notions of being a woman do not bind this framework; non-Native women and those who would like to contribute to the decolonization project can also embrace this framework. Of course it is enhanced and rooted *first* in the experiences of Indigenous women and how they actually live their lives, but it can also be embraced by others as long as they are interested in decolonizing themselves, and acknowledge their relationship to settler colonialism and the liberation of Native people. It is here that I turn to the lyrics of Eekwol, who I think offers a unique potential for expressing an Indigenous hip hop feminist framework.

In the track "I Will Not Be Conquered," Eekwol provides young people with an anthem. She tells them to fight for community and self, to struggle against colonialism. I want to hone in on the second verse, which presents, for me, an Indigenous feminist framework for resisting settler colonialism collectively.

> I don't care if you don't like me
> I don't even try
> My circle includes those wiling to die
> There's a war going on outside
> But you can't see it unless you open your eyes
> Where words are weapons, deadly weapons
> Suicidal syllables submerged in sentence
> Exploding explanations kill the questions
> Listen really hard, learn the lessons
> Protect your rights and your way of life
> For the young and the old who cannot fight[30]

This verse represents an Indigenous hip hop feminist framework in part because her words are about community uplift. While Indigenous feminists are concerned with their own bodies and that of other Indigenous women (i.e., the Missing and Murdered Indigenous Women in Canada), they are also concerned with the development of the entire community. As Cree/Metis feminist Kim Andersen writes, "Indigenous feminism is about honouring creation in all its forms while also fostering the kind of critical thinking that allow us to stay true to our traditional reverence of life."[31] Eekwol challenges Native people to learn their histories and cultures, to open their eyes to what is going on around them. For her, hip hop is the mechanism through which she can not only express herself but also raise awareness about issues in Indigenous North America. If there is a war outside against Indigenous people, we should be thankful we have a warrior with words, fighting as an Indigenous feminist. Beyond her caring words for Native people, she also has a specific track that is, at its core, an example of how Indigenous hip hop feminism might be an avenue through which Indigenous manhood can be restored.

In the song "Protect Us," Eekwol offers a window into how many Native women might feel about Indigenous men today. The term "protect us" is misleading, only in the sense that she is calling on men to return to more progressive forms of masculinity. In the first verse, she gives some uplifting comments for Indigenous men:

> This is dedicated to the men in my life
> Strong on the front line, sharp as knives
> This is for the guys who stay up late
> Worry about family and our future state
> This is for protector, today's dog soldiers
> Walk low crouch with the weight on their shoulders
> Talkin' bout the ones who take care of their kids
> Responsible, givin' them the tools to live
> This is for my homies who focus on the physical
> Mental, emotional, but don't forget the spiritual

She begins by praising those Indigenous men who actively participate in the taking care of their families and communities. This is a direct commentary on the stereotyping of Native men as deadbeat dads who do not partake in the childrearing process. She also gives props to all of the Native men who are constantly engaging in deep thought about how to change their communities. I think this framing allows for Native men to listen so that she can then begin the critical conversation about things Native men need to do in order to better their communities, especially those who are not engaged in community uplift. She asks Native men to also be spiritual. It is not clear if she is telling Native men to return to ceremonies, whatever that may mean for different Native men, but surely it suggests we should reflect on our own selves as Native men and how we relate to one another. After all, relationships to one another are deeply spiritual.

In the second part of the verse, she explains to Indigenous men that she, as an Indigenous sista, understands their struggle, which is historically based. Native men are products of colonialism. She encourages her Indigenous brothas to relearn to fight and struggle, in spite of the colonial baggage of historical trauma.

> Bring back the will and the reason to fight
> Protect us.
> I know my men, you've had it the worse
> History tells us you the raw deal first
> They took away your role
> Along with your soul
> Expect you to succeed
> That's taken its toll
> Where's our protectors, our leaders our fighters?
> Outside the bar holding bottles and lighters?
> Pimpin' us, hatin' us, leavin' us alone
> To fight against the elements that stole the home

Is there room for an Indigenous hip hop feminist framework? Hell, yeah! I think we need to begin to further consider that the work being put in by Native female artists is a form of Indigenous feminism. We can utilize the dope scholarship of black hip hop feminists in order to develop Indigenous hip hop feminist theories that are not essential in nature, but are multifaceted, place the experience of Indigenous women within hip hop and how that is represented, within settler colonialism, race, class, gender, and sexuality.

I want to be careful, though, as a black/Indigenous male. Indeed, Indigenous women can and have always spoken for themselves; my family and all of the Indigenous women who continue to influence me greatly are a testament to that. I am in no way attempting to speak for them. But

it is some shit worth noting, and should be considered for future scholars working in the field of Indigenous hip hop.

In March 2016, my Twitter blew up with criticisms of Onigaming
First Nation (Anishinaabe) public figure Wab Kinew. He was running
for Manitoba New Democrats in Fort Rouge in the provincial election in
the spring of 2016. He had come under controversy for homophobic and
misogynist rap lyrics and tweets. Former federal Conservative cabinet
minister Michelle Rempel called him out, saying his comments are
"inhumane."[32] Noel Bernier, the director of the Manitoba Liberal Party's
northern Indigenous caucus, also directed criticism at Kinew for his
comments, stating that they are "hurtful, they're damaging, and they're
offensive to a lot of people."[33] These criticisms were not just from non–
First Nations people; Native people also criticized him on social media.

Beyond this narrow game of politics, Native women and Two-
Spirit people still feel harm from his comments. He has addressed these
concerns as best as he can in his bestselling book *The Reason I Walk*,
published in 2015. He writes, "I would like to apologize to everyone I
have hurt along the way, physically and emotionally." He mentions that
he was "an angry, self-centered young man," and he prays "this apology
is accepted." Perhaps a sign of maturity, he also apologized for his lyrics:

> I would also like to apologize for misogynistic rap lyrics I have
> written or performed in the past. At the time I thought it was funny
> or had shock value. With the epidemic of violence against women,
> and Indigenous women in particular, there is no excuse for this.
> We have to do better, all of us, and hip-hop musicians can play an
> important part by ending the use of terms, images, and themes that
> degrade or disrespect women. I am committed to doing that and
> encourage other rappers to do so as well.[34]

Many have said that he is only apologizing because he is entering Canadian
politics; that might be true. Some say he is not sincere and this does not
account for his homophobic tweets, which he did not apologize for in
the same paragraph. Regardless of his intentions, there is merit to the
message. Indigenous male hip hop artists do need to be held accountable

for what they say, write, and what images they produce. The people who bear the brunt of misogynistic, trans- and homophobic lyrics are those still most vulnerable in our communities. Leanne Simpson has a better and more practical approach. She writes, "White supremacy, rape culture, and the real symbolic attack on gender, sexual identity, and agency are powerful tools of colonialism, settler colonialism, and capitalism primarily because they work efficiently to remove Indigenous peoples from our territories and prevent reclamation of those territories through mobilization."[35] This approach is both sincere and practical in terms of how Indigenous male hip hop artists should consider dealing with gender violence. Simpson further states, "It's in all our best interests to take on gender violence as a core resurgence project, a core decolonization project, a core of any indigenous mobilization."[36]

In this regard, those of us working in the fields of Indigenous hip hop studies, me included, need to do better ourselves. It is not enough to give big shouts to some of our favorite artists or demonstrate how well they challenge settler colonialism; if they are not lifting up our communities, then we need to check that shit! (I am not a part of the no-fun police; we can still have fun while remaining critical.)

Chapter Four

"HE'S JUST TRYNA BE BLACK"

The Intersections of Blackness and Indigeneity in Hip Hop Culture

Introduction

At the 2004 46th Annual Grammy Awards, hip hop artist Andre 3000 one-half of the hip hop duo Outkast, performed their certified platinum hit "Hey Ya," which won the award for best urban/alternative performance. Though critics lauded the song and performance, it set off considerable controversy throughout Indian Country. Andre 3000 dressed up as an "Indian," and scantily dressed women emerged out of large teepees. He even began his performance, stating in a low voice, "The Natives are truly restless." He then performed the song. While the crowd watched his wonderful performance in awe, Native peoples reacted negatively. It was another example of a non-Indigenous person, in this case a black American, "playing Indian."

I remember watching this performance with amazement and astonishment. I was amazed that I could see the live, television performance of "Hey Ya," one of my favorite songs, done by one of my favorite artists, and astonished that Andre 3000 could so easily play Indian in his performance. I was upset. But so were others, including Cherokee rapper Litefoot.

Litefoot, whose real name is Paul Gary Davis, is a pioneer in the production of Native hip hop. In an interview with allhiphop.com, Litefoot offered an important criticism of Andre's performance. "If I would have dressed up like a Zulu and stuck a bone in my nose and held a watermelon and sang one of my songs that had nothing to do with Zulus," said Litefoot, "do you think that I would have made it out of that auditorium? We all know the answer."[1]

Since entering the rap game in 1989, Litefoot had received all sorts of criticism and racist comments from black Americans such as, "You're an Indian. Indians don't rap." He had also heard people say, "Indians ride horses and live in teepees. Do what Indians do and leave the rap game alone." While he did say that Afrika Bambaataa, a rap godfather, offered support for his art, most had been cold to him, at least early on. Ultimately, Litefoot wanted a simple apology from Andre 3000. He never received one.

The story of Andre 3000's redfacing performance and Litefoot's response illustrates the uneasy tensions between blackness and indigeneity in hip hop culture. Unfortunately, black American hip hop artists continue to utilize indigeneity in their art in a very negative way. T.I. is another example, which I will get into later. I am not saying that they are on par with white folks who engage in the art of cultural appropriation, but I am saying that they would flip out if a Native person dressed up in blackface or rocked a Black Sambo on a medallion or hoodie. We still need to engage in critical dialogues across and beyond the black-white and Native-settler relations.

There are innumerable articles, books, commentaries, and essays that analyze, discuss, and explain the historical roots and contemporary pervasiveness of antiblack racism. There is critical race theory, pioneered by scholars such as Derrick Bell and Kimberlee Crenshaw,[2] racial formation theory written by Michael Omi and Howard Winant,[3] and systematic race theory, explicated by Joe Feagin and Sean Elias.[4] There is black feminist theory and intersectionality,[5] pioneered by the important work of Patricia Hill-Collins and others. And plenty more scholars have theorized about race and racism, including Eduardo Bonilla Silva.[6] Others have written on the development of whiteness studies, both historical and sociological projects. In other words, racism is central to the very core of US democracy. Few scholars, though, while making important contributions to understanding racial theory at large, have included Native peoples and their engagement with settler colonialism as a major part of their work. I have identified a number of scholars in the introduction, including Jodi Byrd, Patrick Wolfe, Glen Coulthard, and also Audra Simpson.[7] Yet, besides Byrd and Wolfe, they tend to focus on

Native-settler relations. For my purposes, I will focus on Indigenous-black relations through the lens of hip hop culture.

There is a long history of black-Indigenous relationships, especially in the United States. I briefly outlined some of this history in the introduction. However, it is worth noting again that black and Native histories have intersected and diverged in unique ways, outside of this traditional scholarship.[8] A part of this chapter's contribution is to add to that scholarship, specifically through the lens of hip hop culture. It is time we find creative ways to reimagine black-Indigenous relationships, cultures, and histories in ways that bring to the fore new scholarship and new understandings not tied to stories of enslavement and dispossession, even as those things are a ubiquitous part of our presence. Hip hop helps us do that in one way.

On the flip side, Native people in hip hop culture engage with blackness in unique ways. For instance, they produce features of Black English within their work, most notably for my purposes, Tall Paul, who utilizes both Black English and Anishinaabemowin in his raps. Aesthetically, they also perform blackness by rocking snapbacks with braids (shout out to Frank Waln), or even as seen in Chase Manhattan's art. He performs a combination of blackness and indigeneity that remains uniquely Indigenous.

Keeping these examples in mind, I ask: What does it mean to be a Native hip hop artist who also engages with blackness? I contend that by engaging with blackness, as performed through hip hop, Native hip hop artists are also defining new ways of what it means to be modern Indigenous people. Through hip hop, Native artists are able to remix representations of indigeneity with blackness, and repackage a digestible form of being Native to their audiences. Importantly, they also challenge myopic conceptions of blackness in a way that respects but also expands the very notion of it.

Indigenous Imagery in Hip Hop Culture: T.I.

Native people have taken up one of the key struggles of our time: ending the harmful and racist mascots that negatively portray them.[9] Amanda Blackhorse (Diné) et al. is a leading plaintiff against the Washington R-word team in the District of Columbia. At the time of writing this, the case is still in federal court. This longstanding struggle has only intensified with the rise of social media; thus, we have a hashtag such as #notyourmascot, which has taken the Twitter world by storm. It has also aided many of us in identifying the long, historical portrayal of Native people, and why we need to do everything we can to challenge racist stereotypes, including shaping public discourse in whatever mediums exist to do so. For me, one of the major contradictions that has yet to be critically analyzed is how nonwhite folks, especially, black Americans, rock the gear of some of these professional sports teams, and what that means for black-Indigenous relations.

Check it: I was in the Raleigh-Durham Airport headed to Chi-Town, flying with Southwest Airlines. While waiting in line for Group B to be called, I saw a brotha in Group A wearing a Hustle Gang shirt (more on this later). It is a shirt that has an Indian chief head; it is the emblem of T.I.'s Grand Hustle Gang label. I had to ask him, "Whas goin' on, bruh. Yo, what does the chief head symbolize on that shirt? I'm Native and was just curious." He responded, "It's just the Hustle Gang symbol, just about doin' you, bein' yourself." I just nodded and said, "Cool." This brief anecdote suggests that many black Americans might be clueless about Native mascots and representations. While they might know a Black Sambo is racist as hell, the real impact of Native invisibility is that it persists even among people of other oppressed groups. It makes me think, "Damn, *they* won, huh?!"

I can hear some of my Indigenous peeps now, "How can blacks wear that? They're no better than white people!" I hear all of that, but there is no need to perpetuate the oppression Olympics.[10] We have different historical experiences, and they might be narrated differently in historical memory, some more than others, but no one group has it worse than others. Although we do need to discuss whatever issues might exist in order to educate one another, what does comparing who has it worse accomplish in dismantling the structure?

I understand Native people's frustration with black people not acknowledging their oppression. Black Americans wearing the gear of racist mascots is inappropriate, and perpetuates stereotypes about Native people and their assumed invisibility as living, breathing human beings. However, it is embedded within a matrix of power and multiple forms of oppression. For one, simply reacting by saying that black folks are no better than white people (or some version of that) only reproduces tension between the groups. For instance, black folks can easily say that Native people held slaves (of course not all Native people, but it is an easy retort), or that the Cherokee Nation has kicked out all of the black folks and is therefore racist. This response is a logical fallacy, but there is not much of a solid comeback. Unfortunately, these stereotypes exist within hip hop culture as well. Therefore, hip hop becomes a site through which we can disaggregate these contradictions, between blackness and indigeneity, because the culture is filled with many contradictions, from positive portrayals of women to misogyny, from homophobia to queer rappers able to utilize hip hop to perform a variety of genders. While Indigenous people have used hip hop, for example, to challenge colonialism, they are involved in a culture that has historically negatively portrayed Native people. From hip hop's formation, anti-Indianness has existed, even as black folks were attempting to showcase some appreciation for historical figures. Now, let me turn to one of my favorite rappers, T.I., and his portrayal of Indigenous people.

Figure 7. Rapper Chase Manhattan aka Mr. Hustle Tribe, rockin the Native bling with the Viking chief head. Courtesy of Chase Manhattan. Used with permission. https://www.instagram.com/p/kfiXJdDLQL/?taken-by=mrhustletribe&hl=en

What is a hustler? A hustler is someone who is fundamentally concerned with competition and survival; they will get *it*—whatever that it might be—by any means necessary. They will turn water into wine in order to make it. They are *about* competition. They compete on the block to sell drugs, to make money, to make a better life for themselves, for "community." Hip hop mogul Jay Z (aka Shawn Carter) described why a young black man begins hustling: to make money and for the potential excitement of adventure and riches. "The truth is that most kids on the corner aren't making big money," said Jay Z. "But they're getting rewarded in ways that go beyond dollars and cents." They believe they are "getting a shot at a dream," ignoring the aspects such as violence and the low pay.[11] But hustlers are not simply hyper-capitalists who are out for self, which sounds selfish. They grew up in areas where you had to survive and no one was going to help. "The competition wasn't about greed or not just about greed. It was about survival."[12] So hustling is about competition, about perseverance, when all odds are against you. Perhaps this is why rapper T.I. has chosen an Indian chief head to represent his hustle. Indians were brave, and they fought to the end. In order to legitimize his hustle, why not use Indians who were conquered long ago? T.I. chose an Indian head because Indians, for him and for the brothas on the block, whom he represents, need Indians to justify why young black men survive against all odds and conquer their environment.

The rapper T.I. has long been called the King of the South. He is the winner of three Grammys, and founded his own label, Grand Hustle Music, in 2003. He has his own television show with his wife, Tiny. He has also served prison terms for gun charges on at least two separate occasions while being one of the most well known artists in the hip hop game. So, what does T.I. have to do with Native peoples? The emblem that represents Hustle Gang headdress is an Indian chief head with a headdress.

Black folks' use of Indigenous images is complicated. Yet there seem to be two possible reasons for it. First, African Americans, like other non-Indigenous peoples, do not know the *process* of Native genocide in this country. While it is common knowledge in black language for African Americans to mention a long-lost Native family member (a common phrase of "I got Indian in me" is used to explain why someone has "good" hair; usually long and straight), they might not know of any Native peoples who have maintained cultural ties to a Native community. Reaching back into the depths of history, we can consider the rhetoric of Malcolm X. The radical Malcolm X, a staunch advocate of black human rights globally, would use rhetoric that rendered Native people and realities invisible.[13] The segregation of African Americans and to an extent, of Native Americans from one another adds another layer to this.

The second reason is thorny. T.I. grew up in Atlanta, home of the Major League Baseball team the Atlanta Braves. Perhaps this makes sense. However, the major reason seems to be T.I.'s affinity for trap muzik. Arguably, T.I. and others popularized the style in the early 2000s. With the major success of his 2003 *Trap Muzik* album, the genre was here to stay. Trap muzik is a southern variety of hip hop music that glorifies sex, drugs, money, and other stories of growing up in the "trap" or the hood. A major aspect of the "trap" is selling drugs and surviving. People are literally trapped under the yoke of racial bondage, and, with little opportunities for upward (or outward) mobility, many young women and men of color end up pursuing a life of crime. And yet, just like hip hop's genesis, trap muzik germinated into something special, in spite of the social conditions.

Maybe T.I. was also making connections between fur trapping and living in the trap, or the hood. While it is difficult to discern what Hustle Gang believes may be the parallels between fur trading (or trapping animals) and trapping in the hood, it can be understood as a metaphor. Fur trading was hard for all involved, and it depleted the animal population; only the strong survived. Hustling is about making better moves than the other people, and surviving. While it can lead to riches for some, the other animals understood as people here can easily be depleted. Those without certain resources, such as intellect and the ability to be the most macho, lose.

Yet, through a critical lens we can see that mostly, the Hustle Gang emblem is redfacing on tee shirts. It is a perpetuation of Native stereotyping. The specific aspects of this redfacing are a play on Indigenous masculinity, at least Hustle Gang's interpretation of it. Indigenous men represent bravery, silence, and are fearless against danger. A hustler in the trap is also supposed to represent these attributes. They are to be brave. Snitching is looked down upon. You must be fearless: you can't be afraid to go to jail, get shot, or deal with the certain forms of death in the hood. The urban black male's fascination with death is not surprising. Cultural theorist Aimé Ellis argues that the death-bound imagination of young black men "is made up not only of the commonly accepted beliefs and market mediated stories about death defiance, glory, and reckless disregard," it is also a "worldview constituted by the seductive certainty *and* uncertainty that a death-bound identity brings within view."[14]

However, both of these ideas remain difficult to support. Although from the hood, T.I. is an internationally known entertainer, who may therefore have access to certain people who can educate him on Indigenous issues. Regardless, he is participating in settler colonialism, specifically the erasure of Native peoples by appropriating a chief logo for his company's brand. We must begin to challenge these stereotypes and come to grips with the fact that black Americans, too, can be just as wrong about a social issue, even if historically they have been on the forefront of racial justice.

Intersections: Chief, Snoop Lion, and "Blowed" and Misogyny

At the same time, it is important to admit that Indigenous people can also participate in negative aspects of redfacing. Failing to do so ignores Indigenous hip hop reality. To simply say that Native Americans do not participate in negative aspects of redfacing ignores Indigenous hip hop reality. For example, the collaborative video between Snoop Lion (formerly Snoop Dogg) and Mohawk rapper Chief reveals the interaction between blackness and indigeneity, in very complicated ways. Snoop engages in stereotypes, while Chief engages in outright misogyny. Here, the plot thickens. We are not talking about the ideal potential of blacks and Indigenous people coming together to destroy colonialism and white supremacy. Instead, we are talking about a Native rapper complicit in both the objectification of Native women and the production of racist stereotypes, while allowing another (black) male to participate in these colonial activities. They do all this in the track "Blowed."

The song has a hot beat. It is about smoking weed, partying, and the conquering of Native women's bodies. At its core, the song is unflattering for Native people at best, and, at its worse, it is denigrating of Native women, plain and simple. To be clear, this type of perspective is not new to hip hop and certainly is not unique to music genres across North America. Nor can we blame hip hop for the denigration of women. Furthermore, while the song does nothing to challenge the fact there are so many murdered and missing Indigenous women in parts of the US and mostly Canada, it cannot be blamed solely for such issues, though it might be complicit. In fact, Chief is engaged in a form of redfacing. Michelle Raheja offers a brilliant definition of redfacing. She writes that early Native American actors performed redface in order to "absorb, deflect, redirect, and placate fantasies projected" on Native Americans by non-Indigenous peoples.[15] In this case and in this moment, when Indigenous people have a variety of platforms to challenge racist stereotypes, Chief is engaging in redface in the negative, reproducing stereotypes where they are unnecessary.

Although the song is Chief's, Snoop starts the track off. He wears a brown fur coat and sunglasses. In the first verse, Snoop makes claim to being an Indian. "Yeees, I'm an Indian, two braids in my hair wit a pipe in my hand." It is faintly followed by the stereotypical [place hand over mouth] "war chant." Chief follows. After mentioning how bad he is in the bedroom, he proclaims himself "Native American royalty/so she feel obligated to spoil me."[16] He continues, "Man that's kush in peace pipe." Apparently the weed he smokes is so potent that "it'll wake Bob Marley up outta his casket." Chief authenticates Snoop's indigeneity by giving him an audience, a public, that directly addresses Native people, and he uses stereotypes to promote his own hypermasculinity of conquering women's bodies. Still, we need to be careful about how we critique and discuss Indigenous rappers, so that we do not use this type of video to then lead us into the field of antiblackness. We should be able to criticize Chief's video as misogynist and stereotypical, without also blaming hip hop, or black culture, for corrupting an Indigenous man.

Chief also celebrates his Indigenous masculinity. The lyrics and representation of women are misogynistic, and, unfortunately, promote a love for smoking weed and celebrating the conquering of Indigenous women's bodies. Six Native women remain in the background during the entire video, wearing eagle feathers, headdresses, and stereotypical Plains buckskin. They are smoking weed in what appears to be a classic Chevy Impala an ode to West Coast hip hop. In the background, images of wampum are projected onto four panels, scrolling down gently to the rhythm of the music. Whereas in the past, wampum was brought to negotiations to foster peace between different Indigenous tribes, this was not the case in the music video.[17]

The song illustrates the apolitical nature of redfacing in this instance. Importantly, in the video, Chief is not performing as an Indian per se; that is, he is dressed in hip hop clothing (Adidas, velour, and a tee shirt). However, the women are dressed in Indigenous garb, with their bodies exposed for the gaze of men's eyes. This makes Chief's claim to indigeneity authentic, but it is through the bodies of Indigenous women. Thus, he authenticates Snoop's indigeneity while also reinforcing stereotypes about Indigenous women. It also represents the limits of hip hop culture.

In hip hop studies, we spend a lot of our energies on showcasing how hip hop helps people around the world find a voice, challenge oppression, and build positive community relations. However, hip hop does not always promote social justice warriors. Hip hop can potentially play a huge role in building black and Indigenous futures of decolonization, but it cannot be the only means by which we accomplish such social transformation. Without attention being paid to patriarchy, it will be difficult to create solidarities for all people in our communities.

Appropriating Blackness in Indigenous Hip Hop

A major theme in hip hop culture is authenticity, or, to put it simply, keepin' it real. A subtext to that idea is who can produce hip hop, and under what terms. Recently, the large, uncategorized social media groups known as "Black Twitter" have taken white rappers to task for what they feel is impersonating and appropriating black culture without give black folks their due. For instance, hip hop legend Q-Tip called out Iggy Azalea for what he believed was a lack of hip hop history. Black Twitter followed suit, and never let up. Black Twitter has not only criticized Azalea but also Taylor Swift, Kylie Jenner, Justin Bieber, and a host of other white artists for appropriating black culture but not saying shit when things like police brutality happen to black folks. What I have always been curious about, though, is whether Native folks can engage in the difficult dynamics of cultural appropriation. Check it: Native people were rightfully upset when hip hop mogul Pharrell Williams posed for *Elle* magazine wearing a headdress. He would later apologize for that mistake.[18] He seemed genuine in his response. But, again, can Native people engage in cultural appropriation like, say, white folks? Yes and no. Here is my rationale.

When you hear Native artists mention their favorite hip hop artists, it is usually someone black, which is cool. They also state that they were drawn to the music because of the stories rappers told about poverty and struggle, something that they could identify with. Poverty and structural racism and colonialism have a funny way of shaping people's realities in very similar ways, even if the details of those histories are particular. That story is not unique people around the world have gravitated to hip hop for similar reasons, primary among them being that it is a way to express their pain and sorrow over living in a cruel world. While some acknowledge and express their deep love and respect of hip hop culture, indeed black culture, many do not, and that is cultural appropriation. I should note that I am not equating Indigenous folks with whites. If I had to create a hierarchy of oppression, whites would not make the top of my list. But cultural appropriation can happen the other way, and it is about time we talk about it.

While Chase Manhattan presents an interesting character of being an Indigenous rapper, he explicitly uses ideas of blackness but remixes it to make it uniquely Indigenous. In the track "#Followmytribe" from of his 2015 album *Warrior DNA*, he states, "Yea I'm dancin' like an Indian/ and I'm lookin' like I'm Mexican/they say I'm rappin' like them blacks again." This is an overt engagement with blackness. He surely believes he looks Mexican to some, likely using some stereotypical view of what a Mexican person is supposed to look like. He still incorporates powwow music and dances into his art, and others are likely saying he raps like he is black. Chase Manhattan is offering a subtle critique: anyone who engages with hip hop is also engaging with ideas of blackness, especially if one raps. As sociolinguist Geneva Smitherman argues, "Rap music is Ebonics to the max."[19] While members of the Native community may make such comments, it is true, and there is no getting away from it. However, as Frank Waln has repeated over and over again, Native people are story-tellers too, and have been for thousands of years.[20] Thus, to engage with hip hop, you use black grammatical features, but you also put your own twist on it. Therefore, Chase Manhattan's "#Followmytribe" is a uniquely Indigenous thing, remixed with a form of blackness.

Chase Manhattan's remixing and use of Indigenous imagery in his work presents some ethical issues for Indigenous hip hop.

Does he help or harm the struggle over the control of how Indigenous images are circulated through mainstream popular culture? On the one hand, he engages in the politics of cultural reappropriation from the settler imagination. On the other hand, he uses these images for capital gain for self. (Yo, Chase, I ain' mad at ya; keep gittin' them checks, homie, as long as we live in this society!) While he does not have a large main-stream following, he does have quite a notable social media presence, and surely Indigenous youth, especially young males, listen to his work and see his imagery on Instagram. But what message is Chase relaying to Native youth? He is telling them to hustle, to focus on their dreams, and to make some money; I can't be mad at that. However, the larger—and perhaps even collective and futuristic—question is, how long can this last, and does it help our communities wrest themselves from the yoke of colonialism? Unfortunately, the message is: you can be Native, perform a uniquely Indigenous masculinity, rock Native bling (I love that shit; it's kinda cold!), and make money. While I am a huge Chase fan, this might not be the best message for youth, especially when main-stream representations are still so pervasive and, subsequently, harmful.

"Y'all Ain' the Only Ones":
Indigenous People Appropriating Blackness

I have already briefly discussed how black Americans and European Americans have engaged in cultural appropriation. When they do this, they perpetuate stereotypes that Native people all look alike, that we all wear headdresses, and so forth. We all know this exists, and Indigenous people have been doing many things to challenge that sort of racism. I want to return, though, to opening up the possibilities of Native appropriation of blackness through language.

Before proceeding, my aim here is not to say that one group has it harder. But if contradiction is the ruling principle of the universe, as Huey P. Newton told William Buckley, then you can have appropriations of blackness that perpetuate stereotypes about black Americans, especially men. However, I do believe that Indigenous people engage in cultural appropriations of blackness in two ways positive and negative simply, good and bad. Let me return to language, especially the work of critical sociolinguist Geneva Smitherman.

Geneva Smitherman (aka Dr. G) has been on the forefront of language policy and championing the rights of black language for decades. By black language, I mean African American English, also called Ebonics; it also has a host of other names. Black English has a history and unique linguistic, grammatical structure from what we might call "White English." (I am not going to spend several pages convincing the reader that Black English actually exists; the data and scholarship is there. As these scholars have articulated for decades, when whites reject Black English, it is not really the issue of language, as linguists have closed that case long ago; it has more to do with how racist some are in rejecting the very notion of a black language. People become irrational and refuse to look at the data. So, if you feel some type of way about Black English, consider reading the notes and then make an informed conclusion.[21]

Black language developed out of one of human history's worst sins: the Atlantic slave trade. According to Smitherman, Black English developed as a mixture of English and West African languages, as a direct result of blacks' enslavement. Of course, it has changed and developed over time. Smitherman provides a succinct definition. She writes that Black English is "an Africanized form of English reflecting Black America's linguistic-cultural African heritage and the conditions of servitude, oppression and life in America. Black Language is Euro-American speech with an

Afro-American nuance, tone, and gesture."[22] Importantly, Black English has two components: language and style. Even more importantly, the major differences between Black English and White English are at the level of grammar. Today, we see that not only is hip hop the epitome of Black English today, many people have adopted it in everyday speech, including corporations.

Language in general, and Black English in particular, can be an important aspect of social change. As Smitherman writes, "language plays a dominant role in the formation of ideology, consciousness, behavior and social relations."[23] If language plays such a dominant role in social relations and ideology, it can be appropriated in both positive and negative ways. Smitherman further writes of language:

> I refer, in a holistic sense, both to language as abstract structure and language in speech interaction, and to a symbolic system rooted in social formations. I view language and speech—that is, individual and social expressions, structure and use—as a unified behavioral dialectic governing the cognitive and social life of [people].[24]

Language, then, is abstract and material. It is a system that also shapes social relations. The language of the hip hop nation also shapes social relations and ideology. Language in hip hop is fundamentally rooted in black languages, especially in the North America context. No matter where in the world hip hop goes, language and grammatical formations go, too. Thus, so does black language.

My thesis is this: to not acknowledge Indigenous appropriations of black language in their rhymes is to engage in cultural appropriation of blackness. I do not think it is a malicious intent, but intention does not mean there is no harm, or, in this case, the erasure of black cultural production in hip hop culture.

Tall Paul and Black Cultural Appropriation: A Positive Approach?

Tall Paul, a Leech Lake Ojibwa rapper out of Minneapolis, Minnesota, presents what I believe is a progressive example of cultural appropriation for the benefit of his people. This does not, therefore, suggest that other rappers talking about the rez are not doing some good, nor am I trying to create a binary between "conscious" and "unconscious" rap. I am, however, trying to bring to bear how Indigenous artists can do some linguistic crossover, appropriating black language in a useful way, for Indigenous cultural sovereignty.

Anishinaabemowin: Promoting Cultural Sovereignty through Language

Revolutionary theorist Frantz Fanon once stated, "To speak means being able to use syntax and possessing the morphology of such and such a language." More than this, "it means above all assuming a culture and bearing the weight of civilization."[25] Culture and language are intimately linked. Rapping is, in fact, a language unto itself; indeed linguists such as H. Samy Alim have called the language production in the hip hop community "Hip Hop Linguistics."[26] The art of rap is a difficult thing to master, and one where your aptitude is measured by your ability to put words together in a skillful, playful, and clever manner. Though there are many styles, rap, like its cultural/linguistic foremother, Black English, remains a counter language that challenges the hegemony of so-called standard American English. Hip hop nation language is a counter language, according to critical sociolinguist Geneva Smitherman because of its rootedness in the black speech community. Moreover, rappers boldly continue "Black America's 400-year rejection of Euro-American cultural, racial and linguistic domination."[27]

Extending Smitherman's argument, if rap is a consistent challenge to centuries of Euro-American cultural and racial domination, this is also true for Anishinaabemowin. There is a lot at stake for the revitalization of Indigenous language. A congressional report titled *Problems Facing Native American Youths* (2003) stated that loss of language was one of the major crises facing Indigenous youth in the United States.[28] Losing a language is a major blow to any cultural group's survival. Though a people can persist, it becomes that much more difficult to pass on stories. There are some who have been active in the fight for revitalizing

Indigenous languages, and rappers can and do play an important role.[29] Because rappers are postmodern orators, they have the capacity to help further the cause of cultural and linguistic revitalization. Hip hop has the potential to not only allow for Native peoples to pass on "traditional" stories, but also to create new ones, in Anishinaabemowin and other languages. Therefore, when Indigenous hip hop artists like Tall Paul utilize Anishinaabemowin in their rap lyrics, they are simultaneously rejecting white linguistic and cultural standards and asserting Indigenous peoples' right to their own language. Tall Paul is, in essence, making his mark in promoting Indigenous sovereignty, and bearing the weight of the Anishinaabeg. Though the track begins in English, the chorus is in Anishinaabemowin:

> *Gichi-Manidoo wiidookawishin ji-mashkawiziyaan*
> (Great Spirit help me be strong)
> *Mii dash bami'idiziyaan*
> (so that I can help myself)
> *Miizhishinaam zaagi'iiwewin*
> (show us all love)
> *Ganoozh ishinaam, bizindaw ishinaam*
> (talk to us, hear us)
> *Mii-wenji nagamoyaan*
> (that is why I am singing)
> *Nimishomis wiidookawishinaan ji-aabajitooyaang*
>   *anishinabe izhitwaawin*
> (Grandfather help us to use the Indian customs/ways)
> *Mii-ji-bigikendamaan keyaa anishinabee bimaadiziwin*
> (so that we'll know how to live the Indian way [the good life]).

There are at least two themes that emerge from the chorus, his prayer, his *mshkiki*: authenticity and reclamation. In the first line, Tall Paul asks Gichi-Manidoo to help him be strong so that he can help himself. But help him do what? He asks the Creator to help him use the Anishinaabeg way of life in order to live as an Anishinaabe. There is a bit of tension in his lyrics, and it is unclear what he means by living the Anishinaabeg way of life. This is a prayer, and he is calling for the Creator to give him guidance. Key to interpreting an Anishinaabeg story is an acceptance that there are multiple meanings, and humans can interact with non-human entities. Anishinaabeg stories "do not rule out the possibility of unmediated interactions with reality beyond the human mind."[30] Though he is using a "modern" artistic/cultural/linguistic medium through which to express his ideas and even praying, he is relaying a story that can be transformative to its listener. How that transformation happens is incomplete, and can change from listener to listener. The important thing is that it is spoken.

Using rap to resurrect one's language is a powerful tool to combat colonialism. Indigenous language revitalization is necessary because of what happened during the boarding school era an epoch in Indigenous-US (and other settler nation-states) history where Native children were kidnapped, taken to boarding schools, and where many were not allowed to speak their language.[31] Tall Paul's code switching between English and Anishinaabemowin is a *mshkiki* for Indigenous peoples. As Métis scholar Dylan Miner observes, "Through the gentle act of speaking . . . Native peoples have been able to maintain intrapersonal communication." Furthermore, "Indigenous languages have also facilitated cross-cultural interchange with other tribal peoples, as well as in the animal plant, and spirit worlds."[32] Part of Tall Paul's

challenge was that he did not feel connected to the spirit world, or Gichi-Manidoo. In fact, he states, "It seems my prayer's weak/I can't speak not a linguist/does he hear my English when I vent?" He does bring up an interesting point about sovereignty, spirituality, and language. To question whether or not his prayers mean anything to Gichi-Manidoo is important. The suppression of language was not only a loss of important knowledge and stories, but also the soul of Anishinaabeg humanity. This reminds me of the words of Coast Salish writer Lee Maracle, who argues that for Indigenous peoples, words come from a sacred place. "The orator is coming from a place of prayer and as such attempts to be persuasive." More than this, the words of orators "represent the accumulated knowledge, cultural values, the vision, of an entire people or peoples."[33] Rapping in Anishinaabemowin is a way to heal the soul and acknowledge the humanity of Anishinaabeg. In other words, he is saying I have a right to my own language, I have a right to live, and I have a right to be human an Anishinaabeg. Though he is speaking of his own experience, Paul is also "narrativizing" for other Indigenous people who might have had similar experiences in urban Minneapolis. Given the precise history of language repression in the United States committed against Indigenous people, to speak in Anishinaabemowin is a defiant act rooted in politics.

Rapping in Anishinaabemowin is a political act. As mentioned above, under the yoke of colonialism, many Indigenous nations have lost fluent speakers of their languages. There are various forms of language revitalization on the ground, though, including immersion schools and language camps. Rapping in two languages allows him to connect to two different audiences, empowering him to directly challenge settler colonialism. He is not only challenging the hegemony of an English-only standard, but also the sole use of hip hop nation language (Black English) within his rhyme schemes. He is creating an avenue whereby Indigenous youth who participate in rapping can find another way (of many) to challenge colonialism and promote sovereignty within Indigenous communities. Tall Paul is claiming "rhetorical sovereignty in the face of daunting pressures to assimilate linguistically."[34]

There is more that can be said about black-Indigenous language crossover in Indigenous hip hop music, and linguists and literacy scholars would do well to begin to analyze such a thing. More importantly, though, Tall Paul might be on to something—something that might change the future of the language problems facing Indigenous communities in the US and other settler states. If hip hop can serve as the anthem of the oppressed, it might also serve as *the* mechanism through which Indigenous languages are not only further resurrected but also maintained. It can produce new worldviews for the future of Indigenous sovereignty, at least one can hope.

I think rap in particular and hip hop more generally can affect change or spark necessary dialogue within Indigenous communities in various geographic settings. It further contests ideas about authenticity and the false modern/traditional binary. But, as Tall Paul demonstrates, it can also serve as a *mshkiki* (medicine) for Indigenous peoples. In my own experience listening to Tall Paul and a host of other Indigenous hip hop artists, it not only serves as a *mshkiki*, it also inspires me to promote Indigenous sovereignty in any way I can. We might consider using hip hop to teach Anishinaabemowin and other Indigenous languages. As Scott Richard Lyons writes, "So let the language activists imbue them with all the authenticities that may be required to get their programs funded, functional, and filled, and let the rest of us see this work as an exercise of sovereignty and support it accordingly."[35] I think hip hop embedded with an Indigenous language has the potential to revitalize languages.

Though some might resist the idea that hip hop can become a sacred realm for healing Indigenous communities, I would not simply dismiss it. It could potentially serve as a path for Indigenous people to work toward cultural, political, and social sovereignty within the settler nation-state. Only time will tell.

Appropriating (Regressive) Black Masculinity

Language is also symbolic. People create meaning through their words and aesthetics. One of the things that bothers me and surely bothers Indigenous artists is when other Native people make comments to them such as, "Why are you tryna be black?" as if hip hop belongs only to black Americans or exists solely within the confines of black cultural expression. It is likely a level of misunderstanding of the fluidity of black culture and its impact on US popular culture in general; it is also a function of cultural appropriation—and it ain' all good. For example, there are what we should call regressive forms of performing black masculinity in hip hop culture. This form of masculinity promotes misogyny and is outright sexist. Unfortunately, Native male rappers often adopt it and do so to the detriment of Native women. Hence, just as when black folks wear headdresses, perpetuating the idea that Native people live in the past and all look alike, which does not help Native people shed colonialism, Native male rappers can perform regressive forms of black masculinity, which does not serve the black community. It perpetuates stereotypes about black men, that all they want to do is make money, hate women, and party. That stereotype is prominent in not only this society but around the world, and disseminated through American culture, as they see hip hop. This does not dissolve settler colonialism and white supremacy as systems of oppression from creating these social conditions, but hey, we can do better amongst ourselves. If we are truly going to change social conditions, we have to be careful in how we not only talk about one another but how we also appropriate and perform regressive forms of, for example, black masculinity, in the public sphere.

Indigenous Contributions to Black Lives Matter

Alicia Garza. Opal Tometi. Patrisse Cullors. These folks—queer black women—are the founders of Black Lives Matter. Lemme repeat that: queer black women founded Black Lives Matter, first in a post on social media, in response to the acquittal of George Zimmerman for the murder of seventeen-year-old Trayvon Martin (rest in power, lil bro, we ain' forgot about you!). If that killing was not enough, they organized in Ferguson, Missouri, after police officer Darren Wilson killed eighteen-year-old Michael Brown (you rest in power too, bro; we ain' forgot about you neither!). It is important to highlight because much of their work gets appropriated and, worse, outright ignored by black men, who utilize very patriarchal notions of liberation that do not explicitly acknowledge and take seriously the contributions and lives of queer and trans black folks. The assertion of Black Lives Matter is that black humanity matters, in a country where it has never mattered. The founders state, "Black Lives Matter is an ideological and political intervention in a world where Black lives are systematically and intentionally targeted for demise. It is an affirmation of Black folks' contributions to this society, our humanity, and our resilience in the face of deadly opposition."[36] They also assert that black women's lives matter, like Renisha McBride and Sandra Bland. Importantly, they also assert that black queer and trans lives matter, too, including the reported, unreported, and mis-gendering of murdered black trans folk; y'all rest in power, too. These lives should be an integral part of any movement toward black liberation. So, props to them.

Recent events, such as the murder of twelve-year-old Tamir Rice by Officer Timothy Loehmann and his partner, Frank Garmback, in

Cleveland, Ohio, among others, have sparked national outrage, especially among black America. And the fact that the prosecutor, Timothy McGinty, refused to indict the officers reveals in a general sense, at least to me, that black lives, in fact, don't matter in a settler colonial and white supremacist society.[37] I would go so far as to say black and Indigenous lives have never mattered (to the state), and if they did, they did only in the sense that it benefitted the state, what the late legal scholar Derrick Bell called "interest convergence." In using this concept, Bell explained why, following the landmark *Brown v. Board of Education* US Supreme Court decision in 1954, schools became more segregated. He argued that the state only decided to desegregate public institutions not because they were so inclined, out of their humanity, to end racial segregation. But rather, the United States wanted to better its image during the height of the Cold War in the eyes of rapidly decolonizing countries, and they could see the economic power that desegregation provided, at least to those in power.[38]

Fortunately, beyond black America, Indigenous artists like Tall Paul and others[39] are contributing to the #BlackLivesMatter movement through song. In the track "No Questions" from his latest album, "No Good Good Guy," Tall Paul, a Leech Lake Anishinaabe rapper from Minneapolis, Minnesota, connects for us, black history and black lives today. He reminds us that the killing of black youth is not new.

What I find unique about his approach is that it is a Native rapper talking about black issues, which is really dope. (I do wonder how many black artists would, in turn, make a track about an Indigenous issue beyond some token reference to genocide.) In order to make my case, I want to juxtapose these texts, which is what I believe Tall Paul is attempting to accomplish.[40] Tall Paul is using two examples of black male killing, constructed through an Anishinaabe male perspective, in order to tell the listener what we might gain from these historical and contemporary examples. In addition, he is offering a bridge to black Americans, where we might be able to gain a coalition for decolonization. After all, both forms of oppression, in a settler regime, exist in parallel.

In this track, he discusses two very different events, but ultimately parallel cases: the killing of a young black male. First, he discusses the detainment and, later, execution of fourteen-year-old George Stinney.

Stinney, in 1944, was accused of murdering two young white girls in Alcolu, South Carolina; he would later die in the electric chair. (In December 2014, Judge Carmen Tevis Mullen would overturn that decision.[41]) He was convicted, under the justice of white terrorism, of murdering those two young girls with a stick. In the first verse, Tall Paul describes the case of George Stinney. Ultimately, he describes the rationale for killing him. The white family needed some closure for the killing of their two girls, so, what do you do when white womanhood is violated? You blame a black male and then kill him, a common trope, which has always had deadly consequences a part of Amerikkkan democracy, as Amerikkkan as cherry pie.

He then discusses the killing of Tamir Rice. Officer Timothy Loehmann killed Rice within two seconds of arriving at the scene. Rice was holding a toy gun. The officer believed Rice was twenty years old. Apparently, being a black child has consequences. It appears that Rice, like Sandra Bland, like Freddie Gray, like Eric Garner, like Mike Brown, was murdered for being black. As poet Claudia Rankine writes so beautifully and painfully, "Because White men can't police their imagination/ Black men are dying" and black women, too.[42] In this track, he explains in one verse how the police, the armed guard of the state, imagined Tamir Rice, a preteen child, a black child.

In the chorus, Tall Paul explains how the all-too-frequent narrative of black killing works: police officers get paid and the child is dead; their family is given no justice. They are left with only the dead body to bury, while the officer walks free, even sometimes getting a raise.

> The light devil gets his name on a shirt
> The dark angel lives in danger then a grave in the dirt
> They're both famous for the way their situations at work
> One's dead one's alive tell me what is it worth
> All light ain't devils, all dark ain't angels
> Being light gets paid, being dark gets fatal
> The system made dark skin synonymous with criminality
> Cops'll pop your dark ass, no questions[43]

What we should appreciate most about this track is that it reveals how black Americans feel when they hear of another black person murdered at the hands of the police. It is okay to kill young black men. The police don't ask questions; they shoot first, even at a child. And then they wait and see what happens, letting the body sit there in cold blood for several minutes. And then the black body is once again made a spectacle; we are forced to see the killing of someone, one of us, over and over; and once more, the state fails us because no one is held responsible. In April 2016, US district judge Dan Polster presided over a settlement of $6 million to be paid by the city of Cleveland to Tamir Rice's family.[44]

Native rappers such as Tall Paul are not only bringing awareness to Indigenous communities about Indigenous issues, but he is also sharing with the world the reality of what it is like to be a black child in the United States. There is no justice, only pain and suffering and, always, the potential to be murdered, because of the color of one's skin no questions asked. Tall Paul presents for us the paradox of US democracy, at least experienced by black Americans: Black lives matter and don't matter, both existing, often, at the peril of black Americans and children. Now ain' that some fucked up shit! In December 2015, a grand jury declined to prosecute officers Timothy Loehman and Frank Garmback, who shot and killed Tamir Rice.[45] Rest in Power, Tamir, and peace and blessings to his family.

#FlintWaterCrisis

Whenever I mention the #FlintWaterCrisis, I first have to say, I am outright and completely biased: I believe Michigan governor Richard Snyder deserves to go to jail for one of the most egregious forms of urban environmental racism we have seen. He willingly allowed Flint's water source to be switched from the Detroit water authority to the Flint River, which is extremely poisonous.[46] Flint has been receiving water from the Great Lakes Water Authority, which took over the Detroit Water and Sewage Department, since January 2016.[47]

Regardless of my personal bias (did I mention I think Snyder should go to jail?), Native people were active participants in challenging the environmental racism that impacted a majority black city. Of course there are Native people living there, too, but many responded positively, illustrating that there is room for black-Indigenous solidarity. Indigenous Detroit hip hop artists were on the forefront in challenging environmental racism in Flint, providing water and making rhymes.

In their track "Pay 2 Be Poisoned," Detroit SouFy (Anishinaabe), featuring ZebrA OctobrA and Lisa Brunk (Anishinaabe), break down the political economy of the crisis, from a Native perspective. On SouFy's Soundcloud website he writes, "This song is inspired by the Flint Water Crisis & the constant fight to protect our water and Indigenous lands."[48] The brilliance of the track is that they did not respond by saying Native people "have it worse" or people are "only talking about this because it happened to blacks," as if Native people did not live in Flint. There were, for example, some newspaper headlines that read, "Flint is Not the Only Water Crisis America Ignored"[49] and "Navajo Water Supply is More Horrific Than Flint, But no One Cares Because They're Native American."[50] These headlines, although certainly meant to illustrate the erasure of Native people and issues, ignored the fact that Native people lived in Flint, too, and just because it is not on reserve/ation land, doesn't mean that Native people aren't also affected. These headlines are more opportunistic than helpful and (though I hope not) possibly antiblack in the sense that they easily dismiss black causes simply for the fact that black issues have and continue to be the dominant discussion of social justice issues (i.e., the civil rights movement and now Black Lives Matter). In contrast, "Pay 2 Be Poisoned" discussed the importance of water for Indigenous people and for residents in Flint, which is a majority black city. The track begins with "True protectors of the water are the women," which pays homage to the Indigenous belief that water, the source of the life, is like the woman who gives birth to children. Children exist first in their mother's womb, surrounded by bodily fluids that help nourish them. But to politicians, not caring for how water impacts those most vulnerable, it is just "sharks eatin' fishes" and simply "big business." To them, it is about making money or "cutting" cost—the neoliberal project of cutting costs without thinking about how these might impact the lives of the poor. They continue,

> They don't think seven generations ahead
> They got knowledge to stop it
> They feed they pockets instead
> See they make the laws then throw you in they prison
> This is why supremacy and environmental racism
> Welcome to America/leave your hope at the door
> Cause Snyder like a sniper with his focus on the poor
> This don't happen in the burbs or where the politicians live
> Wouldn't give that same water to the politicians kid
> They evil doin' keeps us in the ruins
> Tryin' to depopulate we looked at as less than human
> And things getting heavier that's just the light load
> Black labor plus red land equals white gold[51]

In this verse, they articulate Governor Snyder's assaults on the poor and workers in Michigan. Michigan is a "Right-to-Work" state, following Wisconsin, which is a means to wipe out unions in the state. These rappers, being from Detroit, also understand how Snyder works, as he has undemocratically imposed an emergency financial manager over the city's operation, which helped usher in the bankruptcy (the city council correctly asserts that they never declared bankruptcy, which is true; the state did), the largest metropolis to do so. Going back to Flint, they also make a key point: the water of those in the suburbs of Flint was fine. In fact, government officials in Flint were warned in January 2015 that the tap water was unsafe to drink. Therefore, they were given bottled water to drink while at work.[52] We also know from disclosed emails that Dennis Muchmore, Snyder's then chief of staff, told health officials as early as 2014 about the elevated levels of lead in the water.[53]

Perhaps one of the most important parts of the song is when SouFy states that "black labor plus red land equals white gold." This is contrary to those headlines mentioned above, for it illustrates the connections between blackness and indigeneity, or how white supremacy and settler colonialism can operate in parallel, impacting two groups treated differently historically, at the same time. It is also a reminder of that painful history, and a call to action for those folks to get together.

Sacramento Knoxx, an Anishinaabe/Chicanx hip hop artist from southwest Detroit also produced a track on the Flint water crisis. Titled "Nakweshkodaadiiidaa Ekobiiyag,"[54] which in Anishinaabemowin means, "Let's meet by the water," it was a protest song calling those in Michigan and Canada to attend a water ceremony at the Flint River on April 16, 2016.[55]

These two examples suggest that there is some solidarity between artists in hip hop culture. Also supporting Flint citizens were the Little River Band of Ottawa Indians, located in Michigan, who donated $10,000 to the residents of Flint.[56] While many people give lip service, two things show where your heart is: giving money and time. Big props to them, as a sovereign nation, for giving to a city whose residents are predominantly black.

Black Americans and Indigenous peoples have a common experience of oppression living within settler and white supremacist states; there are also many differences that require unpacking. Some of these artists present a certain hope for all of us; that social conditions can change, and we can change them together. Hip hop can help build these new futures, assisting both black and Indigenous people in creating a future of alliance that respects difference but also finds ways to collaborate, together. The next step is to have black folks advocating for, in the mainstream, Indigenous rights and sovereignty.

Chapter Five

RHYMING DECOLONIZATION

A Conversation with
Frank Waln, Sicangu Lakota

Introduction

I first met Frank Waln in Madison, Wisconsin, in October 2015. Nichole Boyd (big shout sis!), coordinator for American Indian Student Academic Services at the University of Wisconsin, Madison, brought Frank and me out as part of the First Wave Program, coordinated by Willie Ney. Check this program out; it is the only one of its kind in the country at a university. And if there are any talented, high school Native hip hop artists out there, please do consider applying.

When I first went up to him, admittedly, I was star-struck. Frank is famous as hell. He was featured prominently on MTV's *Rebel Music: Native America*. He has been interviewed in *Playboy* and *Vibe*; he has nearly 18,000 followers on Twitter. He's big time. In his art, one can feel the love and passion he has for his people, the Lakota, and all other Indigenous and oppressed folks, as well as his deep hatred for all of those things decent people should hate, such as racism, sexism, and colonialism. The cat can spit fire.

When we first met, he graciously gave me dap while bowing his head. I was taken aback. Here I am, a young professor who don't nobody know, and he, a famous artist, is as humble as they come. Nichole had brought us out so that Frank could perform, and so that he and I could do a workshop together. A few weeks prior to meeting in Madison, we talked briefly on the phone about what type of workshop we would do. We both agreed that breaking down stereotypes about Indigenous people was the best thing we could do, because, unfortunately, that shit still exists.

I convened a panel featuring Frank, J. Ivy, Telmary Diaz (a dope Cuban emcee and, as a female, a pioneer in the game down there!), and Baba Israel, an artist from New York City. By the way, Baba can beat-box like a G, seriously. He can freestyle, too. Check him out. Frank and the others performed throughout the weekend in a variety of places, from a middle school to a concert hall.

Frank met with two Menominee youth who are aspiring emcees. I watched him closely. Not in the anthropological sense; it is just in my nature to sit back and observe what is going on around me. He spent the whole weekend mentoring these two young emcees. Little did he know, he mentored me too, someone with a doctorate. I was amazed at how much he simply cared it is not like he did anything special but he just cared so much and encouraged them to pursue their dreams, through hip hop.

On Saturday, October 24, at around 11:00 a.m., Nichole took Frank and me to the Native House on campus. This house is a hangout spot for Native students on UW Madison's campus. It was nice. There were three floors, and a basement readymade for a scary movie. We had brunch with the students, shared laughs, and just had a good time. After leaving the Native House, Frank and I briefly talked about what we would do that day before agreeing that a dialogue with these students and breaking down stereotypes was imperative.

When we got to Overture Hall, he leaned over and said, "You know, Kyle, this is significant: to have a rez Native and a black-Indian historian working together is awesome." Up until that point, I hadn't thought too much about our working together outside of general excitement. But he was absolutely right. Perhaps most notably, we never got into the useless conversation about who is more Native or who has had a more "authentic" Native experience; he simply asked me where I was from, I learned about where he was from, and we moved on. We were both Native, from different parts of the settler nation, and just connected.

We had a blast working with the students. We decided to break the students into groups of three. We asked them to write down two questions they wanted to ask anything they wanted and also to write down one thing they believed to be true about Native American people or histories. The conversation was so stimulating that we went nearly an hour over our allotted time. In fact, Nichole had to shut us down. Later that night, Frank opened up the concert, which was finished by J. Ivy. One of the remarkable things he said before performing "My Stone" was poignant: "The women in my family always told me, 'You don't have to be related to a woman to see her as a human being.'" Wow I thought that a simple but powerful point.

After the concert, I went up to Frank and told him, "I just wanted to let you know, that as a black/Anishinaabe man, as a brotha, I love you." We then embraced in the hip hop fashion with some dap and a half-hug.

What I appreciated most about Frank is that he is a soulful brotha. He loves his people Sicangu Lakota and Indigenous people in general; Frank loves humanity. He loves hip hop and has an incredibly deep knowledge and respect for black culture and history (big shout out for that!), and its potential to help Indigenous communities engage in the practice of decolonization, however each Indigenous community sees fit. While I have analyzed his work throughout this book, I share here an interview that he and I did together. He has a lot to offer in his music, and if you ain' listened to his music, stop what you doin' right now and go check him out! He spits fire!

I asked Frank to conduct an interview with me. We discussed a series of questions, and graciously, given his hectic touring schedule, he responded. My aim in this interview is not to be objective or to give a singular response to what Indigenous hip hop is, but rather to offer a window into larger issues of gender, race, and decolonial love from one artist's perspective. I hope his words will touch you as much as he has touched me. He has the perspective of a seasoned pro at life. So, *chi-miigwetch* (thank you very much), Frank, for your work and perspective.

✦

KM: Before getting into the nitty-gritty of the interview, I gotta know, what does hip hop mean to you? How has hip hop "saved your life," to paraphrase Lupe Fiasco?

FW: That's actually one of my favorite songs; I was just listening to it yesterday. But I really do believe that, personally, hip hop saved my life. It wasn't the only factor, but I think that, coupled with, at the time when I was nineteen, I was very depressed. I was very suicidal. I grew up disconnected from my culture and my language, even though it was there for me to freely participate in. It wasn't illegal like it was for our grandparents. A lot of my generation, we were disconnected because of that suppression of our culture. So, I was going through it; I was suffering the effects of colonialism. I was ready to kill myself. And so at the time, on my rez, suicide's always kinda been an issue. But it was really bad during this time.

If I remember right, we had the highest suicide rate in the world for males aged eighteen to twenty-four on our reservation. And I was in that. Whenever I returned to our culture and ceremonies, and returning to that and listening to our elders, it showed me that suicide wasn't the answer to the questions I had that were leading me to that point. And so that showed me, I can't end my life right now, and I'm here for a reason. And then it was like hip hop music gave me that reason. It was the only thing at that time that made me feel like I wanted to be alive. It was like, sittin' down, and makin' beats, and writin' songs, writin' rhymes was my escape from all of the BS that everyone goes through on the rez, especially where I'm from. It was that escape; it gave me life; it gave me a reason to want to live. It became that catalyst for me to look at my own identity as an Indigenous person.

What does hip hop mean to me? First and foremost, I understand it and respect it as a culture. Not just the music, I respect it as a culture, the culture that it came from. Because I'm Indigenous, I'm Lakota, culture is very important to me, so I'm able to see the importance of hip hop culture. So, first and foremost, for me, personally, it's a lifesaving culture.

KM: "My Stone" off of your first album, Born Ready, is one of my favorite tracks. Though, big shout out for "Oil 4 Blood" and "AbOriginal"—I love those tracks. As you have said before, it was a song dedicated to your mother as a gift. What can this song tell us about how the strength of Native women can still help raise a Native man? In other words, how has being raised by a single mother impacted your development—emphasis on it as an ongoing process—as a Lakota, an Indigenous man?

FW: I'm reading this amazing book called *Zuya* [*Life's Journey—Zuya: Oral Teachings from Rosebud*] by this elder in our community named Albert White Hat Sr. He's lived on our reservation all his life. In the book he's just sharing stories about his life, and about how he's seen our culture, life on the rez, and our people change throughout his life. It's just raw storytelling, untouched by Western editing and a Western lens. He says this is a Sincangu Lakota story from a Sincangu Lakota lens.

In the book he talks a lot about how back in the day, before we were colonized, the women did raise the kids, whether they were man or woman. Of course, men would show boys how to hunt, to show men how to do the things they needed to do to survive, but on a day-to-day basis, it was the women who were running shit and who were raising the kids. I was raised in that type of environment, raised by my mom, aunties, and grandma. I didn't realize that I was being raised in that—that was just normal for me. I thought that was normal until I got a little older and started to recognize that I didn't act or think the way that my other male peers did who might have had father figures or who passed that patriarchy down that affected our people. That's when I kinda realized that I had a unique upbringing, and I guess you could say I was brought up in a way that my people used to live—in that matriarchal environment.

If we really wanna create change in our communities, as Indigenous people, as Native people, I think that our women need to be leading those movements and those changes. And I figure if you just look at history, men, we need to take a step back, I think we've fucked it up too many times, man. As men, yes, we have the tools and the skills that our people need to survive, but as men, we need to be letting the women decide what we do with our abilities. Cause even in my career, that's why Tanaya [Winder] is my manager. I've always succeeded, it seems like my path was always moving in the right direction when women were leading me. It goes back to how I was raised.

If you look back at a lot of movements or progress that happen in our communities, a lot of the unsung heroes were women. They were the ones behind the scenes making sure that things were happening and moving. I think that Native men, we like to get up on the podium and take the mic, and talk this and that, but we really need to reevaluate how we love the women in our communities, and also the type of voice or opportunities we give them within our movement.

That song in particular, at first I was a little bit hesitant to write that song because it's a very vulnerable song and it is a very vulnerable position, especially as a man in hip hop, you know, cause you're supposed to brag about yourself, supposed to say you're the shit. But I understand the history of where that came from as well. And then I was kinda doing this unknowingly, it was just the lens that I was given because these women raised me, because I saw the world differently.

I think it's a statement to have a hip hop song where, as a man of color, you're vulnerable, you're open, you're expressing your emotions, which in my community, the men were taught to not feel, not express our emotions, not love. And that song is very emotional.

I remember I was crying when I wrote it. And it's crazy; I think that energy was captured in that song. Every time I perform that song someone in the crowd comes up to me and say they cried seeing me perform it. So, I think there's definitely a power in that art form. I don't know too many examples where that has been done, where the man is very vulnerable and also speaking on his love for a woman, however that form may be. It's a very human and honest song.

For me, once we get through all of the bullshit of patriarchy, and be honest, and look at, this is what it was, let's just throw all these labels that the settlers and the colonizers and the Western world gave us and look at the truth. The truth is that Native women hold shit down and hold our communities together, they're the reason why we're here, and just speak on it, you know.

I was hesitant, but it was like, you know what, this is for my mom, I'm just gonna be honest and write an honest song about the things we went through and the fact that I wouldn't be here without her.

KM: The parallel to your song is Tupac's "Dear Mama."

FW: That was low key an inspiration. The way Tupac just expressed that love. That kinda let me know that that could be done. Even though I kinda did a different flavor, I don't think I woulda been able to write that song without those tributes to mothers that came before. It kinda showed me that, yeah, it can be done.

As Native men, we need to reevaluate the way we love women and how we treat women; it's just being honest with yourself. A lot of issues in myself, and again, I'm not perfect, and I'm still unpacking the baggage that comes with being a man. Even though women raised me, I'm not free of those patriarchal influences. I'm still unpacking that. But just being honest with yourself, being honest with the people in your life, being honest with your story, just being honest with the reality that you live.

KM: You have a great deal of respect for hip hop, a black cultural product (and Latin@). In fact, you told me that Nas' "One Mic" is one of your favorite songs (among many, but you mentioned that one). How did you come into hip hop, and how can hip hop, a black art form, become meaningful for a Native kid on the rez (and is still influencing Native kids on reservations everywhere)?

FW: It was inevitable, I came into [hip hop], from my generation, everyone was exposed to it. One of the contributing factors was representation. I know representation is important. All of the representations I saw of Native Americans on TV, and all media platforms, they were so fake, they weren't even close to the realities we were living. My older cousins were listening to hip hop, and once I started hanging out with them, and started paying attention to the music, and I was like, "Holy crap, they're talking about what we're living on the rez." And I think that's why my cousins gravitated to it, and a lot of youth on our reservation. We found comfort in it. It was one of the few things that represented us and what we were living through.

There are a lot of parallels in those stories in hip hop and what we were living on the rez. It was just kinda inevitable. I was around it, and then there was just this power to it. I was just drawn to the storytelling; storytelling is in our culture. I was just drawn to the power of the music, drums, the emotion in it; the way these artists were just being who they were, and speaking on their home and their reality with no filter, and they were just putting it all out there. It was very liberating for me to find those songs. It was like comfort.

I was driving home last night and I was listening to "Music" by Erick Sermon. It's got that Marvin Gaye sample, man, this song just feels like a hug, no matter what mood I'm in, this song just feels like it hugs me. Damn, man, hip hop was pretty much my father. I didn't have any father figure, so hip hop hugged me and made me feel better. Hip hop was like my father. It makes you feel good, something you can't describe.

What's cool is that those two Menominee boys we saw in Madison [Wisconsin] are a testament to that. Hip hop is a young culture. It's very fresh. My generation was the first generation where I'm from making hip hop on our rez. That's cause the school got the grant for the laptops, the MacBooks, and a lot of 'em didn't go back. We had Garage Band and we started recording at home, that's fresh and fairly new. My generation was the first on our rez making hip hop on the rez, and my peers, now, are having kids, so there's gonna be a lot of young Native babies being raised on hip hop, and I think those two young boys are a testament to that; they're gonna be bringing it even harder.

I was raised on country. I wasn't raised fully immersed in the music and the culture from the time I was little, it came later on. Almost every rez I go to, there's almost always two or three rappers in the crowd, young boys and young girls. They wanna be singers, they wanna be rappers, they wanna be dancers, and it makes me happy because the young age that I see these kids and they're performing already, and they're writing songs, and they're performing and they're rapping, they're a lot better than I was at their age. And here I am, getting to travel the world and do what I do. And I think the next couple of generations, there will be a wave of some dope Indigenous hip hop artists.

Also, to keep that connection between the community that created hip hop and now these Indigenous communities that have picked it up and added another flavor to it. I think it's important that as Native people, we understand and respect it, both black and Latino culture. Understanding the roots of the culture, remembering the root of the culture. As Native people, culture is important to us, and giving hip hop the respect that we give our culture.

KM: #BlackLivesMatter has taken the United States by storm. Arguably, it is one of the most important social movements of the twenty-first century. Indigenous people have continued struggling against colonialism, including the building of the Keystone Pipeline. Importantly, it is documented that Native Americans are more likely to be killed by the police than any other group, and yet they receive little to no mainstream attention. In fact, there is a #NativeLivesMatter movement, too. I have three questions. 1) What do you think are the similarities between black oppression and Indigenous oppression in this society? What do you think are the major differences? 2) What are some of the issues affecting Native people (on and off of your rez)? How does your music try and reflect that? 3) Related to the last question, if there were a few things that you would like to share with black Americans who may or may not know anything about Native struggles today, what would you like to share?

FW: I don't have all the answers; I'm still living every day. One of the biggest similarities is that we're fighting against the same system that did this to our people. For our Indigenous people it was genocide; for black people it was slavery, exploiting their labor. That system put us in this position of poverty and also, just being poor, there's also similarities there.

I grew up on the rez out in the middle of the country of South Dakota, but when I moved to Chicago, I started meeting young black and brown people who grew up in poor communities, in the ghettos, there were similarities, even down to stuff like we all ate hot chips, we all used paper plates and plastic forks and plastic cups. There's definitely similarities and just the reality of being poor and being held down by this socioeconomic jail and these borders that they put us in. There are similarities in that.

I think I was out in New York City one time, and I was doing this show, and this young black cat I knew out there and he was like, "Yo, man, the rez is pretty much, from what you're saying, is like a ghetto in the middle of nowhere." I was like, "It kinda is man, we are just in the middle of nowhere." So, I think that there's similarities in that, to live in poverty and it's the same system that held us down.

We also need to acknowledge the differences. We can't just say, "Oh, it's the same," because it's not. But I think it's important that we find that common ground, because that can be where we meet, in the middle, and kinda see that, yes we do have similarities, and be like, damn, we really do have to work together because they're fucking us all over; this system is fucking us all over.

There's so much you can speak on. I'll try and get overall and get down to the specifics. One of the biggest things that my music speaks on and tries to counteract is just the erasure of Indigenous people in all forms in the United States, whether that be in the media, in history, even in social justice movements. They forget about us because we've been erased. We've been erased from the American psyche. Just trying to counteract that erasure with my story, just being honest. And just saying, "Yo, I'm a young Indigenous person, here's my story." Fortunately, now I have this platform, this voice, this following. And just always reminding people that there's this whole history here that they're missing, and I also think that history is important because if we want to speak on the history of the country then Indigenous people need to be a big part of that. We were a big part of it.

I would say another one that I try and speak on and, again, I'm going through them myself, is the lateral violence that we have as Native people. Whether that be the way we hurt each other or people in our communities or the way we look at other people of color, and how we might perpetuate things like antiblackness. We may even be perpetuating settler colonialism, by how we act or the way we think.

Another big one, especially on my album, is depression and suicide. I lived through that as the part of the story about how I'm healing from that. So, erasure, lateral violence, and healing from those colonial wounds.

KM: How can we as Native men create alternative forms of masculinity that are not oppressive and detrimental to our communities?

FW: If I had all of the Native men in front of me and they're down to do whatever, I would say the number one thing we need to do, everything we think we know about being a man, we need to throw it out the fuckin' window. Everything we've been taught is from this Western lens and this culture of patriarchy that's infected our people and that runs this country. We need to throw all of that out the window and start from the ground up and start from our cultures, and whatever that culture may be.

Personally, I'm turning to that book the elder, Albert, from our community wrote. He talks a lot about what being a Lakota man meant before we were colonized, before the church, before alcoholism, before all of these things changed. So, we need to start from ground zero and start from our respective cultures. And also, damn, just listen to our women. Ask them what they think. Just shut up and listen for once!

Once you just get rid of all the bullshit and the smoke screens and the lenses, it's like, damn, it is really simple; it's just hard to see.

I think the song "My Stone," and there will be several songs on my [upcoming] album, that will help us reevaluate our understanding of patriarchy within our communities. Start from our culture; reevaluate our masculinity or what it means to be a man. Look at it through the lens of our respective cultures; bring that into hip hop, write songs from that source.

I was talking to Baba Israel the day after the concert [in Madison, Wisconsin]. We were talking just about hip hop, and he made a good point: he said one of the great elements about hip hop is that you can bring to it who you are. It creates this space and this culture where you can be who you are, no matter what that is or where you're from or what you look like. It gave young black and brown people a space just to be themselves.

I think there's awesome potential there for us Native people to bring our culture and our worldview into that; write songs from those perspectives. It'll make for a really unique perspective, and I think it'll be really fresh. Personally, that's what I'm trying to do and hopefully that's what other Indigenous artists will do, if they choose to. I think as Native hip hop artists, when I was young, I listened to Nas and stuff. When I first started writing I was thinking, "Do I need to write the same songs that I see on TV, or what?" That was the time you could have a Nas or an Outkast or a Missy Elliot or a TLC. There was commercial hip hop that also had some dope messages that were catchy. And I think the industry has kinda squeezed that out and not allowed space for that anymore. So, I think as Native hip hop artists we need to see that for what it is, and realize that we don't always need to be what we see on TV or what we hear on the radio. That isn't the only pathway to success, even though that's what [sic] this music industry that's ran by white dudes in suits is telling us.

KM: You've expressed to me that some people in your community and outside have given you shit for rapping. They might say shit like, "Why are you doing that black thing?" In what ways do you think hip hop and Native culture(s) intersect and complement each other? How does your art bridge Native histories and present realities into something digestible for elders, youth, and even the haters?

FW: How I respond, a lot of times, especially elders, and this is also understandable, all they think they know about hip hop is what they see on TV or hear on the radio; that's only a small aspect, tip of the iceberg to the culture. So, I explain that to them that hip hop, as a culture, is very stereotyped in mainstream media the same way Natives are as a culture. So, when you see Natives in mainstream media, it's a very specific, narrow lens, a narrow view of who we are as a people, of who we are as cultures.

So I say that hip hop gets the same type of treatment from the mainstream media. I say that their notion of hip hop is wrong, and there's a whole spectrum of different types of music of artists, it's a culture, there's all these different elements. I try to educate whenever that happens. But, to me, that statement is antiblackness. I think that whenever that comes up, hopefully, by me explaining, it initiates those conversations that we need to have in our communities, that Native people address the antiblackness that exists in Indian country.

I would say that another way that I'm trying to bridge that gap is by including the elders in even the creation process with what I'm doing. You hear the songs from my new album, and I have commentary from elders. I didn't finish the song yet [for my new album], I recorded one of the most respected medicine men from our tribe to say a prayer in Lakota for the youth on our reservation that I'm gonna put on the album. For me, that's really exciting and I think there's a lot of potential there, for us young Indigenous hip hop artists to include our elders in our art. Bring them in and show them, sit them down and be like, no, this is what it is, let's create this song. And I think that's a way to bridge that gap; include them in the culture, bring them into hip hop and show them what it is.

I think it's not so explicit in saying, "Yo, we're antiblack," cause I'm not there yet. There's definitely moments in lyrics on my album where I allude to that. But I also recognize that as a young Lakota person who grew up in the conservative, Republican, racist state of South Dakota, where it was pretty much just white people and Indians, I'm still also learning and unpacking the antiblackness that I was taught growing up in a place like that. I think moving to Chicago and being able to travel and also being able to experience these different communities through my music and through hip hop, has shown me these blind spots. I'm still unpacking in myself.

But I think that what my music does is, it bridges that gap, and gives us that space so we can have that conversation, but I think that's as far as it is right now. But I think the next step, once you get people in that space, Native elders there, Native people in that space of hip hop, I think our workshop that we did was a really dope example. Just got people in the same space, and sit them down, and talk this shit out. That's the only way it's gonna work out. Personally, I don't think these types of things can be talked out over social media. But once you're sittin' there with a person or you're in the same space or you're seeing a concert, it's a lot easier for that dialogue or that communication or that understanding or that empathy to happen. So, I think, right now, my music just brings us to that space. And I'm still unpacking that myself.

Artistically, one of the elements I wanna bring in is initiating those conversations. Once I get the Native people who are following to that space, where they realize that hip hop and essentially black people aren't what they think they are, and then hopefully next, initiating those conversations.

KM: What words of wisdom would you offer to young, aspiring Native artists and intellectuals who might be ready to give up on pursuing their goals?

FW: One of the lessons I've learned, whatever you may be trying to do, you need to work on it every single day. I worked my ass off, and I'm still working my ass off. You work at something so much you almost become a master at it. It isn't gonna happen overnight. Even when we're coming up in these systems that oppress [us]. You have to work if you wanna survive. That was something our ancestors had to do. If we didn't work, the tribe wouldn't survive. If you didn't go out and hunt, your family would starve. If you didn't know how to put up the tepee, your family would die. So we have to work to survive and hold each other down. That's definitely a big lesson.

Another thing would be to trust your heart. Listen to your heart, and trust it. For a lot of my life, when I was first starting to make this music stuff happen, in my heart, I knew that's what I wanted to do. And in my heart, deep down, I knew I could, but everyone around me was telling me I couldn't and I was listening to them instead of my heart. Once I started listening to my heart, the path showed itself to me, found me, the stars aligned, and that, combined with a really hard work ethic, and working at it every day, and taking every opportunity that came my way has definitely led to my success.

Specifically for Native people, I would also add, be proud of who we are and where we're from. And I encourage Native people to return to our ceremonies and culture. It made me a better person, it's what saved my life, what continues to save my life. But also, find that thing that makes you a better person, that gives you hope. For some people it may be the church or for some people it may be ceremony, whatever that may be, I'm not telling you what to do, but just find that thing that makes you a better person, that gives you hope, especially as Native people. It's really easy to lose hope, with the type of circumstances that we grow up with.

And, I would also add, we focus so much on goals, I would focus more on lifestyle. I know back when I was on the rez, it was like you had this goal, you wanna do music for a living you wanna tour, but it seemed so far away. And that shit was like, damn, man, am I ever going to get there? I don't even see a pathway to get there. If you focus more on lifestyle, you can be like, okay, well, what lifestyle do I want? I wanna be able to make music, I wanna be happy, I wanna do what I love, and you can start that today. You can change your lifestyle today.

Whereas a goal may contribute to the hopelessness cause it may seem so far away. A friend of mine gave me a good analogy: instead of saying how you want the plant to grow, and drawing a picture of this tree, that you want to have, you can instead mold the vase or the pot that it will be growing in. Even that is an Indigenous way of approaching a career or goal. Approach it from your own culture, define your own success. The pathways for the American dream that exist out there, they don't exist for us.

KM: I consider you a historian. How does history impact your music, and how does that turn into challenging racist stereotypes.

FW: I had this really cool revelation. It was the first time I went to New York City, it was 2012, I did this residency with this nonprofit hip hop art forum in Spanish Harlem. It was called High Arts. It was run by this Puerto Rican dude, a New Yorker, a hip hop head, born and raised. We linked up; he was just a New York hip hop head. Through running that program he actually got to go out; he spent some time on the Pine Ridge rez, and he's seen the communities I come from.

One thing he commented on that made me look through a topic, that I didn't even realize before. He was amazed at the way that Lakota people talked about history, our ancestors, like they were still alive today. He said he never saw that before. Where we talked about the history, the present and the future like it was fluid like this. It was something that wasn't a long time ago. We told these stories like they happened today.

That comes out in my music because that's the environment I was raised in. I can't speak for all tribes, but in our culture things are very fluid. It wasn't so compartmentalized, sectionalized: this is history, so it's in the past. We understood that we were living history, and that our ancestors are with us, and that history is with us, and it influences us now. That's probably why that element comes into my music in that environment where things like history and our ancestors are treated like they are alive today, and breathing and influencing how we look at each other. And I think that's a very Lakota thing.

I don't know if you saw the tweets I did yesterday, I'm paraphrasing, yo, white Americans, this whole country is a handout. When your ancestors got here, Native people had to show them how to live here. America is a handout to you. What rights do you have to talk about poor black and brown people wanting fifteen dollars an hour? Whenever you wake up you're living in a handout. And people were really pissed off.

I feel like if you're just speaking the truth, and the truth is in that history, it's gonna counter that narrative. I'm just being honest. These are facts. I didn't make this shit up. There's nothing to be afraid of. Criticism doesn't bother me, as long as there's truth. Not being afraid to speak that truth. It started with me unpacking my own baggage. That now gives me a place to speak on the truth of history in an effective way, and not be afraid on what that would do to the norm or shape things up. I think just by bringing that history out, and Native people, we're very good at it, it's so natural for us to tell these stories, and to tell this history, it counters that narrative that exists about America and Native people, because that history was erased, but if you just speak that truth and we all know, it's gonna show people that they don't know shit about us.

White Americans only want to believe the history that they know. We are that history and reminder that they don't want to own up to or acknowledge. Just by telling that truth we are countering that narrative that is America.

Conclusion

"IT'S BIGGER THAN HIP HOP"

Toward the Indigenous
Hip Hop Generation

Throughout this book, I have tried to explain what it means to be Indigenous today, through hip hop culture. Related to that, I have also tried to argue that Indigenous hip hop provides for us an opportunity to reimagine how we understand the complexities of Indigenous identity production; how we can challenge colonialism, heteropatriachy, and white supremacy; and how hip hop provides a space where Native people, especially youth, can be modern and construct identities not tied to colonialism. I have tried to place Native hip hop within the social realities in which it exists. Indigenous hip hop is here to stay, and is without a doubt the most important and potentially useful cultural movement in Indigenous North America since the 1960s and 1970s. Admittedly, it is hard to conclude such a book, given the unstable nature of hip hop, and not try to place limits on where the fields of Indigenous studies and hip hop studies might go; I will go there anyhow. First I will explain areas of future research. Second, I will offer some brief musings about projects we might consider within our Indigenous communities and Indigenous studies.

Indigenous Hip Hop as Hip Hop Studies

Hip hop studies, like the settler states of Canada and the United States, has an Indigenous erasure problem. As mentioned throughout this book, Native erasure, and its ongoing effects, is directly related to settlers' need for land. How do you take away land? You attempt to kill them off—genocide—and then you imagine them off of the land. While hip hop has its internal contradictions when it comes to gender and representation, we need to add indigeneity, as a category of analysis, to the equation. Here are a few ways we might do this.

First, we need more positive coverage of Indigenous people in educational curriculum and mainstream media coverage. People need to learn that Indigenous people still exist, and most of us do not wear headdresses. None of us look like that racist mascot in Washington, D.C. Before Indigenous hip hop gets its proper due, and hopefully it can aid in the struggle for Indigenous sovereignty, we need to continue to struggle for positive representations of Native people in the mainstream media. It is not about making diversity more palatable for white people; it is about respecting difference, and centering Indigenous experiences in the North American historical and contemporary consciousness.

As far as giving Indigenous hip hop more coverage, we need more "texts" (I mean this broadly) on Indigenous hip hop. As I mentioned in chapter one, I am heartened by the curriculum attached to the *Rebel Music: Native America* documentary. It was an excellent contribution, and we need more. At the same time, we need not reproduce ideas of Indianness that feed into settler fantasies about what being an Indigenous person looks like or means. The one thing I have learned in writing this book is that, at times, we need to let Native-ness just *be*, and see how it develops. In other words, as Native people, we simply need to be who we be. We need mainstream news coverage, blogs, academic and popular books and articles, and podcasts on contemporary Indigenous popular culture (there are many, such as Indigenous science fiction and folks like Vincent Schilling who talk about hip hop). These do exist and are increasingly being released.

Going forward, an important project for the future of Indigenous hip hop is to document the history more carefully. If you casually search "hip hop documentaries" on YouTube, dozens will pop up. Though they are not all equal, most have documented, video evidence of the key moments and histories of the most important cultural movement in the postwar era. We know of how DJ Kool Herc and others started hip hop. We know the Caribbean, West African, black American, and

Latinx histories. We can easily learn about Tupac's murder, race, and gender in hip hop; I believe we need more of this. But we do not have a robust history of Indigenous hip hop's many origins. We need to know the multiple origins of the culture. Where did it come from? Who are the "founders"? How do we tell these competing stories in a digestible narrative for a wide audience? These questions remain, and one of my goals as a scholar of Indigenous hip hop is to continue to document it in a variety of ways, and to make it accessible to both Indigenous and non-Indigenous audiences.

We just need more coverage. We also need more documentaries that follow the lives of Indigenous hip hop artists as they relate to the larger cultural movement. Hopefully, younger folks coming up in the age of social media and more advanced technology will find creative ways to educate the public through one component of Indigenous cultures—hip hop.

My goal in this book has been to use accessible language that pays respect to the Indigenous hip hop community, hip hop studies, and a general educated audience. Some of these projects should also be inter-active, perhaps akin to Jay Z's *Decoded*, where multiple artists choose a song, you can listen to it, and you can also *hear* them explain what each line means throughout. That sort of text might be totally digital, but could reach a younger market of folks who might spend hours trying to decipher the lyrics of some of their favorite Indigenous hip hop artists.

There needs to be more analysis about the relationship between African American language and Native languages, and how they inter-act in rap lyrics. In public talks on Indigenous hip hop, I say this often: whenever Indigenous artists engage in hip hop, especially rappin', they are inevitably engaging in the linguistic-cultural production of blackness; we call this African American language. As Indigenous language revitalization occurs throughout the Indigenous world, we should strengthen the links between Indigenous language revitalization and hip hop culture. Some may balk at that suggestion, arguing that we should not blend these two cultures, but if I have proven anything in this book, it is that Indigenous hip hop is one of many manifestations of contemporary Indigenous cul-tural production, and, at times, utilizes black cultural aesthetics, and language, to achieve that goal. Doing this will require someone to have a deep understanding of three languages: African American, an Indigenous language, and likely a European language, depending on the geographical location. It is a study worth doing, and something that people have already done in other languages.

While I talked about Indigenous masculinity earlier in the text, more work needs to focus on the Indigenous female, trans, and non–gender conforming artists. For instance, we should take notice of Anishinaabe artists like Gabriel Guiboche, also known as Strife Asaakezis, of Winnipeg, Manitoba, who is a Two-Spirit artist.[1] He recently came out as Two-Spirit, along with his partner, Mary Black. This is an important move, and hopefully the youth can learn from artists like Guiboche. Just like we need more work in Indigenous gender and sexuality studies more generally, we could use more work on their experiences in Indigenous hip hop culture in the mainstream.

We still need works that unpack the role hip hop plays in the lives of young people throughout Indigenous communities, in and off of the reserve/ation. Remember, the majority of Native people live in urban areas, and we cannot discount the urban (black American) cultural impact on the clothing, linguistic, and other choices of many Native artists and youth. While many of these artists make fashion uniquely Indigenous, there is something to be said about the intersections of blackness and indigeneity that need to be acknowledged and explained, otherwise we run the risk of engaging in cultural appropriation of black culture.

Fifth, a comparative approach to Indigenous hip hop is needed, and questions abound. Why did Indigenous people in Australia and New Zealand turn to hip hop? What artists influenced them the most? How does hip hop impact Indigenous social relations today? This approach would take some time conducting research in North America and the Pacific. Researchers would need to do oral histories, ethnographic research, and engage in the developing scholarship in global Indigenous studies, similar to the work of Chadwick Allen's *Trans-Indigenous* methodologies.[2] Shit, lemme get some grant money and get to werking…

The Move toward an Indigenous Hip Hop Generation

As a trained historian with a deep love, respect, and appreciation for time and popular culture, I want to turn to the work of cultural critic and journalist Bakari Kitwana. Kitwana wrote more than a decade ago about the hip hop generation, which he described as "young African Americans born between 1965 and 1984 who came of age in the eighties and nineties and who share a specific set of values and attitudes."[3] For Kitwana, one of the major things that signified the uniqueness of this generation of black youth who created and were raised with hip hop culture is globalization.

Beyond the specifics and limits of his framing, he left us with an important point: "The younger generation must understand that no matter how grand our individual achievements (achievements built on gains from past struggles), they mean very little if we cannot overcome at least some of the major social obstacles of our time, leaving a formidable foundation on which the next generation can stand strong."[4] Many times, fueled by generational rifts between activists such as those currently existing between the Black Lives Matter movement activists and those from the civil rights movement generation, the younger folks believe older folks are living in the past, holding onto those past glories, while the older generation seems to think young folks are ungrateful for the price they paid for the little bit of freedom young folks enjoy today— emphasis on "little bit."

We have yet to overcome major issues in our own time, including police brutality, the murder of black trans folks, women and men, the prison industrial complex, the lack of quality education, and climate change, to name only a few, even as many activists are working toward ending these oppressions. Regardless of the ongoing tensions that surely spring forth in every generation, we should remember the past, not to be tied to it, but to learn from it, and carry it with us as we move into new, unknown territories of oppression and contradictions that previous generations did not have to face. Simply put, let us learn together because we do not live on this earth just for ourselves, but for the generations following us. We might consider the current generation of Indigenous activists, artists, and youth as an Indigenous hip hop generation.

If there is a (black American) hip hop generation, surely there is an Indigenous hip hop generation. In the spirit of Kitwana, I also want to suggest that the Indigenous hip hop generation must, in the words of decolonial psychiatrist and theorist Frantz Fanon, "discover its mission, fulfill it or betray it, in relative opacity."[5]

There are several factors that define the Indigenous hip hop generation, and key among them is the quest for sovereignty.

We still have pipelines to protest throughout Turtle Island. Under the regime of President Forty-five, we still have to fight the construction of the Dakota Access Pipeline, which, following a rerouting, now has oil being pumped across Standing Rock Sioux land. (At the time of this writing, President Forty-five has fully supported the pipeline, and oil is going through. I am glad that water protectors, and my homies Nick Estes, Melanize Yazzie, and Jaskirian Dhillon, are still writing and protesting on this issue.) There are also pipelines being constructed near my neck of the woods, in the Great Lakes, and also in Pacific Northwest.

We need better human and nonhuman (animals and plants) relations. (Big shout to Zoe Todd and Kim TallBear; I've been learning so much from you two!) We need to reclaim Indigenous place names (the homies Susan Blight [Couchiching First Nation] and Hayden King been putting in work in this regard up in the 6ix).[6] We have many battles to fight, so let me name just a few more.

Combating Youth Suicide

The first is an epidemic impacting Native youth across North America today: suicide. As a researcher, I was inclined to put some data in here to prove that it is a problem. Frankly, I do not want to. Take this one case. My heart broke reading the news coverage of the Attawapiskat First Nation (in northern Ontario) youth suicides that occurred in April 2016.

On one Saturday in that month, eleven First Nations youth attempted suicide. Attawapiskat declared a state of emergency. Overall, 101 people have tried to take their lives since September 2015.[7] I shed legitimate tears after reading about that community and those young folks.

We can get into all of the fancy language of what caused each individual problem, but the cause is plain, simple, and systemic: those youth attempted suicide because they are products of colonialism. I am not one who usually accepts simplistic cause-and-effect scenarios, but when eleven youth do it (not to mention the long-standing problem of Indigenous youth suicide in general), that is systemic. In the United States, Native youth, especially boys between the ages of ten and fourteen, are the group most likely to take their own lives,[8] suffering from what Maria Yellow Horse Brave Heart and Lemyra DeBruyn refer to as historical unresolved grief and historical trauma.[9]

A part of this generation's calling is to find ways to end this epidemic, because the settler state will not. There are people doing this work, no doubt. However, if done well, hip hop can serve as a rite of passage and a restoration of progressive masculinities and gender performances; we would do well to implement programming to make this happen. I would love to work with Indigenous hip hop artists who believe in love, are anticolonial and antiracist in perspective, and want to imagine and build a future free of oppression for our youth. Holla at me and let's make this shit happen.

Urban Indigenous People Are Indigenous, Too

Another factor that impacts Indigenous people in general is urbanization, and the effects—positive, negative, and in-between—that living in cities has on the life of young people. Let me be clear about two things: as an urban Indigenous historian, with at least three urban cultural influences, I want to make sure that readers recognize that Native people and cities are not incompatible. As such, you cannot understand the development of modern North American cities without understanding the role of indigeneity, both as a discursive tool and as a claim to land through the dispossession of Native people.[10] Second, while many Native folks in the nineteenth century were removed from their ancestral lands that *became* modern Canadian and US cities, and subsequent generations came back to those altered urban spaces (in part, due to government policies), not all Indigenous people left. While it is hard to trace Indigenous presences in some cities as they developed into their modern forms, indigeneity existed.[11]

According to the 2010 US census, nearly 80 percent of Native people live in urban areas. According to the 2006 Canadian census, more than half of the First Nations population live in Canadian cities, and most of those live in five cities: Calgary, Edmonton, Toronto, Vancouver, and Winnipeg.[12] Given this data, we still be actin' like all things Indigenous operate on reserve/ations, and that "real" Natives live only on the rez. Native people live on the rez, but they live in cities too, and until we embrace the variety of ways Indigenous youth produce cultural, social, and political identities, we run the risk of boxing them in, and not allowing them to carry on the "tradition" of producing Native identities no matter the time period or space in which they live. We just need to "be easy" and let Native youth live. We have already seen, tangentially, how hip hop and urban black culture has impacted the culture of young people. Therefore, we should embrace it, and consider how the urban impacts Indigenous cultures, as they do actually exist.

We need to reclaim urban spaces and declare them as Indigenous spaces. Straight up! As more and more Native people remix urban spaces and engage with a variety of cultures, we must also understand that Native people are evolving people with unique cultural practices that influence and are also impacted by others; I hope we can all be okay and stop the nonsense about how much Indigenous culture we lose just because we decide to live in cities. I see living in a city as an opportunity to expand and grow our various Indigenous cultures as we have always done. Adding to our cultures from others is the epitome of being Indigenous; to ignore that history, and act like we ain never done changed is, in fact, anti-Indigenous.

Missing and Murdered Indigenous Women, or #MMIW

Another central factor is how Native women, trans, and those who inhabit multiple genders are treated within our own communities. They are, as Marc Lamont Hill observes, "Nobodies," that is, those most vulnerable to state-sanctioned violence.[13] The missing and murdered Indigenous women in Canada and the continued forms of violence, both discursively and literally, in the United States is a problem that we must continue to fight. Native people are working on this issue, but the State needs to do more to make sure that Native women have a right to live and be free— of oppression and the possibility that they might be killed just because they are an Indigenous woman.

Men have a responsibility in all of this. I do not mean that we as "men" try and "protect" our women, as if they cannot protect themselves. I do think, however, that we have a responsibility to help our Indigenous sistas and communities, and many times that requires that we work on ourselves in order to establish better social relations between each other. We have so much work to do, and the work can take many forms.

One thing in particular we need to work on is the "macktivist" who is always trying to struggle and then snuggle with Indigenous women and queer subjects. Let me be more direct: Indigenous brothas and even Two-Spirit folks (mostly the brothas) who, while surely serious in their fight for social justice, also use these moments of anger to take advantage of those around them. I'm not referring to a situation where two adults are vibing and shit happens, and it is consensual; cool, y'all is grown. But we all know those men who (like pariahs), at conferences, ceremony, and powwow, will use the language of social justice, but who do not seek to implement it except in their own personal, social relations. Decolonization means becoming better people, and not taking advantage of those most vulnerable in our communities. It also means reimagining sexual relations that are not based on dominance and oppression. If Indigenous women and Two-Spirit folks do not feel safe with their brothas, how can we, in good conscience, reproduce that in so-called safe spaces? Let that sink in.

Revamping and Restoring Indigenous Masculinity

Indigenous masculinity needs restoration. Michi Saagiig Anishinaabe writer Leanne Simpson writes, "Gender violence is central to our ongoing dispossession, occupation, and erasure, and indigenous families and communities have always resisted this. We've always fought back and organized against this—our grandparents resisted gender violence; our youths are organizing and resisting gender violence because we have no other option."[14] I hope people take these words seriously. We need to imagine an indigenous masculinity rooted in today's realities—not what happened 150 years ago. I want to emphasize that I do not mean to say we should not recall important parts of our history, but we must also respond to contemporary conditions as they are, not as they used to be.

A major part of challenging the rampant violence against Indigenous women is also resurrecting the broken forms of masculinity in Indigenous communities. The whole community cannot thrive with only one ful-filled part. Big shout to Kim Anderson and Rob Innes for all of the dope shit that they've been doing on Indigenous masculinity. Big shout also to the many Indigenous women, non–gender binary, and Two-Spirit folks on social media who call out toxic masculinity. We need more efforts like that, and Indigenous men need to respond better when Indigenous women, etc., call us out by acknowledging that particular criticism, and then not do it again. Instead of framing how we need to resurrect Indigenous masculinities in terms of "returning to traditional" notions of masculinity as if Indigenous masculinity was static back in the day we should look at a variety of masculinities within and outside of Indigenous communities. We can take what we need and sift out the negative components. It will take work, but, hey, we *need* to do this; like now.

Actually Walking with, beside, and, at Times, Behind Our Indigenous Sistas

We need the continued work of Indigenous feminists in and outside the academy. It would be even better if we continue to blend them. I appreciate the work and the firestorm that Métis scholar Zoe Todd created in their wonderful essay "An Indigenous Feminist's take on the Ontological Turn: 'Ontology' is just another word for colonialism." Them white philosopher bros is still mad about that. Todd is a wonderful colleague and a brilliant intellectual. Thanks for the work that you do. I also appreciate the important writings of Nehiyaw intellectual Erica Violet Lee. They both force men, including me, to challenge toxic masculinity. *Miigwetch* and much respect, homies.

Sometimes, us men just need to sit back and let others lead the way. We do not always need to be in the spotlight; nor do we need to come up with the best ideas. We should learn to listen to everyone in our communities, and work together.

Activism

For me, the defining component of the Indigenous hip hop generation has been and continues to be activism. Activism can take many forms, so I do not mean to say that marching in the streets is the only way to get shit done. Actually, we have been marching so long, we should wonder what impact it has, assuming that the settler state adapts, too. I have been a proud black-Native person observing the wonderful work of people like Dr. Adrienne Keene (big shout!), the leaders of #IdleNoMore (big shout Jessica Gordon, Sylvia McAdam, Sheelah McLean, and Nina Wilson; much love), Amanda Blackhorse, Tara Hauska, Susan Blight, and a host of other Indigenous people, I am grateful for all of their work. I have also been inspired by the current (at the time of this writing) collective work of water protectors at Standing Rock, who continue to resist the construction of the Dakota Access Pipeline: #NoDAPL!

Native people from across Turtle Island and throughout the Indigenous world have resisted the $3.8 billion Dakota Access Pipeline, which was to be built near unceded Standing Rock land, and threatened to contaminate their water source—the Missouri River.[15] While the resistance at Standing Rock is about the environment, it is mostly about Standing Rock sovereignty; that cannot be overstated.

Water protectors have put their bodies on the line to protest the building of the pipeline. Hip hop music has provided another source of resistance. Just like in Flint, hip hop has served as an avenue to resist the black snake, a code word for pipelines and their predilection to spill and contaminate—indeed darken—the water source.[16] Sacramento Knoxx, an Anishinaabe/Chicanx artist from southwest Detroit, while at Standing Rock, created a dope track to protest the Dakota Access Pipeline.

In the track, "Get Back Black Snake," Knoxx articulates a vision of resistance anchored in Indigenous feminism. Indigenous feminism is not just a theory but also "a practical engagement with contemporary social, economic, cultural and political issues."[17] Knoxx begins the track with audio of an Indigenous woman speaking at the November 15, 2016 Day of Action, which honored the Missing and Murdered Indigenous Women. In the speech she says, "Water is life. Women are life givers. We carry the water of life in our wombs. We are precious and we are sacred." While there are some critiques of this narrow version of feminism, it does, however, center the important point of Indigenous resistance in the future: Indigenous women have always been and will continue to be those who lead the struggle against all forms of colonialism. And culture plays an important role in Indigenous resistance. Indeed, as Indigenous feminists Shari Huhndorf and Cheryl Suzack argue, "While activism aims to accomplish material social change, culture fosters critical consciousness by attending to the meanings of history and social relationships and imagining political possibilities."[18] Being the product of Saginaw Chippewa women (big shout Aunt Judy!) who challenged settler colonialism and heteropatriarchy in Detroit, I know firsthand that Native women have always played a significant role in social transformation in our nations and communities, and culture has always been a part of it. This track is not just an ode to the water protectors at Standing Rock but to the Native women in particular. And at the time of this writing, "Get Back Black Snake" has actually gotten back.

Furthermore, a variety of Indigenous hip hop artists went to Standing Rock and held a Mni Wiconi (water is life) benefit concert on November 25, 2016, which was held at Standing Rock High School. Artists in included Tall Paul, Frank Waln, and SouFy. After the pipeline was said to be rerouted in early December, many from the hip hop world, including Chance the Rapper, Talib Kweli, and Pharrell, expressed their jubilation for the resistance that took place at Standing Rock.[19] Their tweets suggested that they were impressed with the activism. To all of these black artists showing love to Indigenous water protectors, and their subsequent victory: respect. And from that perspective, the resistance and victory at Standing Rock should not illustrate the end but rather the beginning of a long fight ahead, especially with Forty-five now serving as the United States' president. We must continue to resist, by any means necessary.

As a black-Indigenous brotha, with the utmost love and respect for their work on behalf of all of us and for the greater humanity, I say *miigwetch*. It would be easy to highlight all of the Indigenous men who do work, and props to them, but these women and non–gender conforming folks, in the fighting spirit of the ancestors before them, deserve all the credit in the world. The resurgence of Native activism, the struggle for the power to define Indigenous humanity and representation, and the centering of gender and sexuality at the heart of these social movements—both resurrecting the past and fighting for the generations that follow us—will be the defining component of Native communities for decades to come. As I have come to know from my own family's activism, men might get the credit, but that don't mean they was the ones doing the work of liberation.

Black-Indigenous Alliances

I am invested in the work of decolonization as it relates to black and Indigenous folks for several reasons, but mostly because I am black and Indigenous. For decolonization to actually work, and by decolonization I mean a return of Indigenous land and an end to the exploitation and murder of black and brown bodies, we need to form alliances between black and Indigenous communities. I think Stokely Carmichael and Charles Hamilton's chapter on "the myth of alliances" in *Black Power* (1967) is still useful for that type of discussion. We must understand our commonalities and differences, study our unique histories, where they have diverged and overlapped, and figure out from there how we can help each another. But all of this has to come from a place of love. While it has been useful that Black Lives Matter—the most important social movement currently happening—attended the protest of the Dakota Access Pipeline, we do need more of this collective action. We should ask, as longtime activist-intellectual Angela Davis has, "But now, how do we talk about bringing various social justice struggles together, across national borders . . . ? How can we really create a framework that allows us to think about these issues together and to organize around these issues together?"[20]

I do not have all of the answers, but I have some. First, I think my Canadian and US black sistas and brothas must reject the uncritical use of the word "decolonization" if it doesn't consider Indigenous people. While black folks surely experience systemic forms of racism, you really cannot call yourself colonized in these settler spaces unless you engage with the reality of settler colonialism; that is paramount. Antiblackness in Indigenous North America has to stop. Period. How can you exclude the political and social reality of black folks living here in North America, when many folks' ancestors didn't come here on their own? What did Malcolm X say, "We didn't land on Plymouth Rock, the rock was landed on us." If decolonization means excluding black folks, especially Afro-Indigenous folks because we have adopted white supremacy, then that is not helping at all. We need to deal with that head-on.

The Language of Settler Colonialism:
Or, Policing Indigenous Identity

I think it is time to have a frank discussion about the politics of blood, belonging, and authenticity. Hip hop can challenge what I am calling the "Decolonization of Settler Colonialism." Let me explain what I mean. I am informed by James Sledd's very underrated essay, "Bi-dialectialism: The Linguistics of White Supremacy." He wrote this piece as a reaction to bi-dialectialism, the idea that Black English–speaking students should learn to code-switch to so-called standard English in hopes of assimilating underprivileged black children into whitestream US American culture and educational institutions. He argued that this fundamentally upholds white ways of speaking, and, subsequently, white supremacy. He writes, "The basic assumptions of bi-dialectialism is that the prejudices of middle-class whites cannot be changed but must be accepted and indeed enforced on lesser breeds."[21] He continues, "but white power will deny upward mobility to speakers of black English, who must therefore be made to talk white English in their contacts with the white world."[22] By catering to the formal workings of US colonialism, including federal recognition, we are perpetuating our own demise. We are in a time where, by engaging in colonial forms of recognition, we are sure to do what Yellowknives Dene political theorist Glen Coulthard describes: "reproduce, the very configurations of colonialist, racist, patriarchal state power that Indigenous peoples' demands for recognitions sought to transcend."[23]

We engage in colonial discourses about who belongs and who does not belong to Indigenous communities, based upon imposed colonial logics. There are exceptions, and big shout to Indigenous lawyer Gabriel Galanda, based out of Seattle, who has been fighting against tribal disenrollment in Washington State.[24] Also, I cannot forget the work of David Wilkins over the last twenty years or so and, more recently, the work of White Earth Anishinaabe scholar Jill Doerfler, who, along with others, have helped bring an end to blood quantum in their particular tribal nation as a determinant of Indigenous citizenship.[25] But we should be able to do two things at once: fight colonialism in a big-picture sort of way, and also find more creative ways to include people who have some relationship to an Indigenous community. We should ask ourselves a simple question: In our current views of citizenship, how would our ancestors view it, and how are our children and their children going to maintain their identity as tribal citizens?

As Scott Richard Lyons writes, "As two sources of Indian meaning, both federal recognition and stereotypes produce the kinds of Indians that the dominant society ultimately approves of, because both in turn legitimize the dominant institutions in our society."[26] What I think Lyons is saying is pretty straightforward: you can't decolonize shit until you stop reproducing what the dominant society said and continues to ultimately determine, i.e., what is an "Indian." If you can talk about how well you know your people, all of the ceremonies you attend, how well traveled you are on the powwow circuit, and how "traditional" you are, you should be the biggest voice for those suffering disenrollment. You be wanting white folks and black folks to be good allies, whatever that word means, but you can't be an "ally" to those in your own community doubly suffering under colonialism?

We continue to engage in the fruitless project of identity policing. I am not talking about those who are "pretindians" or those who uncritically appropriate being "Indian" for financial or political reasons. I am talking about how we police identity about who belongs. When speaking with and learning from a variety of Indigenous hip hop artists, most are not interested in asking whether or not you got a tribal id or whether you attend ceremony. I am not saying there are not divisions between "full-bloods" and "mixed-bloods" in various communities, but a lot of people are trying to survive and recover that sweet decolonial love that will help us "git-ovuh." Hell, quite frankly, we need a new way of talkin', one that rejects the colonial politics of recognition but also ethically engages in the politics of belonging. Instead of policing blood quantum or wasting time talking about who is and who is not Indian or Indian enough, or traditional and nontraditional, we should engage in a politics of inclusion and recovery.

I do not suggest that we engage in the neoliberal discourse of multiculturalism, where you try and integrate and then expect people to conform to white standards of everything; after all, as Kim TallBear argues, blood for Native folks does, in some ways, help others identify you. I mean that decolonization requires a commitment to love, not hate, a commitment to compassion, not cruelty. Not every Native person has a neat story about how they have belonged to a community since time immemorial; hell, we can barely get Native people who are white-coded to talk about their privilege in a US context where the phenotypes of race get black and brown bodies killed, literally. Race matters; even skin tone. While you are out championing Indigenous causes and being hyper-Indigenous, don't forget you live in a white supremacist society; those of us darker-skinned folks would appreciate some assistance in calling out white or lighter-skinned privilege, even amongst Native people, for, ultimately, a decolonial now and future. (Big special shout out to Adrienne Keene, Zoe Todd, and Kenzie Allen for talking about this on their social media spaces; much respect!)

Hip Hop Indigenous Pedagogy: A Way Forward

Hip hop can play a central role in all of this. In my short career, I have had the great opportunity to meet and talk with lots of people about hip hop, history, Indigenous Detroit, and a host of other subjects. Out of many of these conversations, I learn of the dope things that hip hop artists and those beyond hip hop are doing. Though they might appreciate me, one of the many frustrations I hear are the disconnects between the academy and hip hop. That is, can hip hop maintain its counterculture roots without being co-opted by some academics who, quite frankly, don't give a damn about the people who produce the culture?[27] What I hear in this statement is this: How does your work as an academic contribute to those outside of the ivory tower? In some ways, this is a fair question. We do have a responsibility to the people who produce the culture. I believe we should advocate for an Indigenous hip hop pedagogy.

Indigenous hip hop pedagogy combines a respect for Indigenous people, cultures, and social reality with using hip hop cultures and texts. It is firmly rooted in the history of Indigenous peoples and their struggles against settler colonialism; it is a call to explore how Native people use and can use hip hop in practical ways. Theoretically, I draw from a variety of recent educational theories scholars who seek nothing more than the transforming of schools; they also are pushing for a radical reimagining of how education works. For instance, I am influenced by educational scholar Django Paris's culturally sustaining pedagogy (CSP), which builds on Gloria Ladson-Billings's culturally relevant pedagogy of the 1990s. Paris argues that CSP "has its explicit goal of supporting multilingualism and multiculturalism in practice and perspective for students and teachers." In addition to this, CSP's goal is to "perpetuate and foster . . . linguistic, literate, and cultural pluralism as part of the democratic project of schooling."[28]

I also draw on the Indigenous studies of education scholars Teresa McCarty and Tiffany Lee, who not only call for a culturally sustaining pedagogy, but ask us to expand Paris's concept to include Native peoples' fight for sovereignty; they call this culturally sustaining/revitalizing pedagogy (CSRP) given that we live in a society in which Native lives are hardly visible.[29] CSRP has three parts. First, they argue that the goal of this pedagogy should be to transform the "legacies of colonization." Second, they contend that CSRP should be to "reclaim and revitalize what has been disrupted and displaced by colonization." Finally, they call for a "community-based accountability." I also want to give a big shout to Eve Tuck and K. Wayne Yang: decolonization ain' no metaphor.[30] If we are serious about decolonizing educational spaces and land, then we must take this seriously, and hip hop is one way to do it.

This pedagogy has to be rooted in the particular spaces in which you find yourself. Indigenous cultural roots, in a broad sense, should be based upon the belief in viewing Native people as they actually live, not some myopic view of how "traditionally" Indigenous people lived. It must also be based upon the belief in creating new components of Indigenous culture for the future generations, and provide youth with the tools to do that on their own. They need not rely on "traditions" alone; but remember and know their history, in order to bring it forward with them as they find new ways to struggle for Indigenous sovereignty.

Is hip hop the best way? I do not know. But can it help? Yes, it can. Hip hop artists do not confine themselves to the limits of today; they try and define how they want to be, and also imagine new futures for the entire Native community. See, through hip hop, you can, at least for a moment, go beyond racism, sexism, homophobia, and colonialism. Hip hop is a way forward, to help us create Indigenous futures, by any means necessary. Indigenous hip hop has the potential to be on the forefront of radical imaginings and help with decolonization efforts across Turtle Island—and beyond.

I hope you had fun reading this book; I know I had a blast writing it. *Bamaappii* (until later).

NOTES

Foreword

1. For the full rundown of Trump's anti-Native stances, see: https://www.washingtonpost.com/national/donald-trumps-long-history-of-clashes-with-native-americans/2016/07/25/80ea91ca-3d77-11e6-80bc-d06711fd2125_story.html?utm_term=.e1b03a853314.

2. http://www.globalpossibilities.org/trumps-order-silence-alaskan-native-voices.

Preface

1. Geneva Smitherman, *Talkin and Testifyin: The Language of Black America* (Detroit: Wayne State University Press, 1986), 2.

2. For style, Smitherman uses black idiom, "It bees dat way sometime." She writes, "Here the language aspect is the use of the verb *be* to indicate a recurring event or habitual condition, rather than a one-time only occurrence. But the total expression—"it bees dat way sometime"—also reflects Black English style, for the statement suggest a point of view, a way of looking at life, and a method of adapting to life's realities. To live by the philosophy of "it bees dat way sometime" is to come to grips with the changes that life bees putting us through, and to accept the changes and bad times as a constant, ever-present reality." (3)

3. Geneva Smitherman, *Word From the Mother: Language and African Americans* (New York: Routledge, 2003), 16.

4. H. Samy Alim, *Roc the Mic: The Language of Hip Hop Culture* (New York: Routledge, 2006). See also Alistair Pennycook, Awad Ibrahim, and H. Samy Alim, eds., *Global Linguistic Flows: Hip Hop Cultures, Youth Identities, and the Politics of Language* (New York: Routledge, 2009).

5. Arthur Spears, "African-American Language Use: Ideology and So-called Obscenity," in *African-American English: Structure,*

History and Use, ed. Salikoko Mufwene et al. (London and New York: Routledge, 1998), 226.

6. Ibid., 232.

7. Ibid.

Introduction

1. Matthew Theriot and Barber Parker, "Native American Youth Gangs: Linking Culture, History and Theory for Improved Understanding, Prevention and Intervention," *Journal of Ethnicity in Criminal Justice* 5, no. 4 (2007): 83–97.

2. Hilary N. Weaver, "Urban and Indigenous: The Challenges of Being a Native American in the City," *Journal of Community Practice* 20 (2012): 479.

3. Donald Fixico, *Termination and Relocation: Federal Indian Policy, 1945–1960* (Albuquerque: University of New Mexico Press, 1986); Donald Fixico, *The Urban Indian Experience in America* (Albuquerque: University of New Mexico Press, 2000); Nicholas Rosenthal, *Reimagining Indian Country: Native Migration and Identity in Twentieth Century Los Angeles* (Chapel Hill: University of North Carolina Press, 2012).

4. Coll Thrush, *Native Seattle: Histories from the Crossing-Over Place* (Seattle: Washington University Press, 2007); Kyle T. Mays, "Indigenous Detroit: Indigeneity, Gender, and Race in the Making of a Modern American City (unpublished manuscript); Colleen Boyd and Coll Thrush, eds., *Phantom Past, Indigenous Presence: Native Ghosts in North American Culture and History* (Lincoln: University of Nebraska Press, 2011).

5. US Census and Canadian Census.

6. Michelle Alexander, *The New Jim Crow: Mass Incarceration in an Age of Colorblindness* (New York: The New Press, 2010); Rhonda Y. Williams, "Something's Wrong Down Here": Poor Black Women and Urban Struggles for Democracy," in Kenneth L. Kusmer and Joe E. Trotter, *African American Urban History Since World War II* (Chicago: University of Chicago Press, 2009), 316–36.

7. Raymond J. Demallie, "The Lakota Ghost Dance: An Ethnohistorical Account," *Pacific Historical Review* 51, no. 4 (1982): 385–405.

8. Glen Coulthard, *Red Skin, White Masks: Rejecting the Colonial Politics of Recognition* (Minneapolis: University of Minnesota Press, 2014).

9. Tricia Rose, *Black Noise: Rap Music and Black Culture in Contemporary America* (Middletown, CT: Wesleyan University Press, 1994), xiv.

10. Ian Condry, *Hip-Hop Japan: Rap and the Paths of Cultural Globalization* (Durham, NC and London: Duke University Press, 2006). See also Tony Mitchell's edited collection Tony Mitchell, *Global Noise: Rap and Hip Hop Outside of the USA* (Middletown, CT: Wesleyan University Press, 2002); Sujatha Fernandes, *Close to the Edge: In Search of the Global Hip Hop Generation* (London and Brooklyn: Verso, 2011).

11. H. Samy Alim, Awad Ibrahim, and Alastair Pennycook, eds., *Global Linguistic Flows: Hip Hop Cultures, Youth Identities, and the Politics of Language* (New York: Routledge, 2009).

12. Jeff Chang, "It's a Hip Hop World," *Foreign Policy* 163 (Nov.–Dec. 2007): 64.

13. http://hiphopdx.com/news/id.11528/title.bun-b-to-teach-course-at-rice-university. Accessed September 27, 2015.

14. See for example, Neal Ullestad, "American Indian Rap and Reggae: Dancing to the 'Beat of a Different Drummer,'" *Popular Music & Society* 23, no. 2 (1999): 62–90; Bret Lashua and Karen Fox, "Rec Needs a New Rhythm Cuz Rap Is Where I'm Livin'," *Leisure Sciences* 28 (2006): 268–283; Marianne Ignace, " 'Why Is My People Sleeping': First Nations Hip Hop Between the Rez and the City," in *Aboriginal Peoples in Canadian Cities: Transformations and Continuities*, ed. Heather Howard and Craig Proulx (Waterloo, Ontario: Wilfrid Laurier University Press, 2011); George Morgan and Andrew Warren, "Aboriginal Youth, Hip Hop, and the Politics of Identification," *Ethnic and Racial Studies* 34, no. 6 (2010): 925–47.

15. Alan Aquallo, "Without Reservations: Native Hip Hop and Identity in the Music of W.O.R." (University of San Diego, 2009); Karen Recollet, "Aural Traditions" (Trent University, 2010).

16. S. C. Watkins, *Hip Hop Matters: Politics, Pop Culture, and the Struggle for the Soul of a Movement* (Boston: Beacon Press, 2005), 247.

17. Jeff Chang, *Can't Stop, Won't Stop: A History of the Hip Hop Generation* (New York: St. Martin's Press, 2005); Watkins, *Hip Hop Matters*. Raquel Rivera's, *New York Ricans From the Hip Hop Zone* (New York: Palgrave-Macmillan, 2003) makes a crucial intervention by highlighting the contributions of Latinx, especially Puerto Ricans, to hip hop culture.

18. Craig Harris, "Divas, Hip-Hoppers, and Electronic Dance Masters," in *Heartbeat, Warble, and the Electric Pow Wow: American Indian Music*, 209–28. Norman: University of Oklahoma Press, 2016.

19. Jeff Berglund, Jan Johnson, and Kimberli Lee, eds. "Introduction," in *Indigenous Pop: Native American Music from Jazz to Hip Hop*, 4. (Tucson: University of Arizona Press, 2016).

20. Gail Mackay, "A Reading of Eekwol's Apprentice to the Mystery as an Expression of Cree Youth's Cultural Role and Responsibility," in *Indigenous Pop: Native American Music from Jazz to Hip Hop*, 201–23. Tucson: University of Arizona Press, 2016.

21. Tony Mitchell, "Blackfellas, Rapping, Breaking and Writing: A Short History of Aboriginal Rap," *Aboriginal History* 30 (2006): 124.

22. Jeff Chang, "Native Tongues: An Interview with Cristina Verán," Internet, July 5, 2006. http://www.pbs.org/pov/borders/2006/talk/jeff_chang/000317.html.

23. Carter G. Woodson, "The Relations of Negroes and Indians in Massachusetts," *The Journal of Negro History* 1, no. 5 (1920): 45.

24. Sharon P. Holland and Tiya Miles, "Afro-Native Realities," in *The World of Indigenous North America*, ed. Robert Warrior (New York: Routledge, 2015), 529.

25. Paul Gilroy, *The Black Atlantic: Modernity and Double Consciousness* (Cambridge: Harvard University Press, 1993), 2.

26. Jace Weaver, *The Red Atlantic: American Indigenes and the Making of the Modern World, 1000–1927* (Chapel Hill: University of North Carolina, 2014), 17, 32.

27. John W. Troutman, "Steelin' the Slide: Hawai'i and the Birth of the Blues Guitar," *Southern Cultures*, Global Southern Music (September 2013): 26–52. See also his first book, *Indian Blues: American Indians and the Politics of Music, 1879–1934* (Norman: University of

Oklahoma Press, 2009). He also has a forthcoming book titled *Kika Kila*: *The Hawaiian Steel Guitar and the Indigenization of American Music* (Chapel Hill: University of North Carolina Press, forthcoming).

28. Manning Marable, "Blackness Beyond Boundaries: Navigating the Political Economies of Global Inequality," in *Transnational Blackness*: *Navigating the Global Color Line*, ed. Manning Marable and Vanessa Agard-Jones (New York: Palgrave Macmillan, 2008), 7.

29. Ibid., 4.

30. Ibid.

31. Mark Anthony Neal, *Soul Babies: Black Popular Culture and the Post-Soul Aesthetic* (New York: Routledge, 2002), 3.

32. "Declaration of the Rights of Indigenous Peoples" (United Nations, 2007).

33. Maile Arvin, "Analytics of Indigeneity," in *Native Studies Keywords*, ed. Stephanie Nohelani Teves, Andrea Smith, and Michelle Raheja (Tucson: University of Arizona Press, 2015), 119–21.

34. Joy Harjo, "We Were There When Jazz Was Invented." http://www. dukecityfix.com/profiles/blogs/the-sunday-poem-joy-harjo.

35. I use language here in the Bhaktinian sense. See Mikhail Bakhtin, *The Dialogic Imagination: Four Essays*, ed. Michael Holquist, trans. Caryl Emerson and Michael Holquist (Austin: University of Texas Press, 1981).

36. Rose, *Black Noise*, 2.

37. Ibid.

38. Smitherman, *Talkin and Testifyin: The Language of Black America* (Detroit: Wayne State University Press, 1986), 2.

39. See Geneva Smitherman, *Word From The Mother: Language and African Americans* (New York: Routledge, 2003), 15–18. According to Smitherman, linguists do not really care much about whether a speech community has a language or dialect; that seems to be the mainstream issue. When it comes to African American language, the issue is more of a political one, and dare I say, one of racism.

40. Geneva Smitherman, "The Chain Remain the Same: Communicative Practices in the Hip Hop Nation," *The Black Scholar* 28, no. 1 (September 1997): 4.

41. Scott Richard Lyons, "Richard Scott Lyons, "Rhetorical Sovereignty: What Do American Indians Want from Writing?" *College Composition and Communication* 51, no. 3 (February 2000): 449–50.

42. Kyle T. Mays, "Promoting Sovereignty, Rapping Mshkiki (Medicine): A Critical Anishinaabeg Reading of Rapper Tall Paul's Prayer's in A Song," *Social Identities*, special issue (in press).

43. Jodi Byrd, *The Transit of Empire: Indigenous Critiques of Colonialism* (Minneapolis: University of Minnesota Press, 2011), 54.

44. Jean O'Brien, *Firsting and Lasting: Writing Indians Out of Existence in New England* (Minneapolis: University of Minnesota Press, 2010); Philip Deloria, *Indians in Unexpected Places* (Lawrence: University Press of Kansas, 2004); Jace Weaver, *The Red Atlantic: American Indigenes and the Making of the Modern World, 1000–1927* (Chapel Hill: University of North Carolina Press, 2014).

45. Beat Nation http://www.beatnation.org/index.html. Accessed April 3, 2012.

46. Robert Warrior, *Tribal Secrets: Recovering American Indian Intellectual Traditions* (Minneapolis: University of Minnesota Press, 1995), 123.

47. Today, there are numerous Indigenous people challenging mainstream representations of Native people through film, literature, music, art, comedy, and a host of other mechanisms. One of the best, more "modern" representations of this is Cherokee scholar Adrienne Keene's blog "Native Appropriations." She brilliantly responds to any form of cultural appropriation. Check it out here: http://nativeappropriations.com/. Accessed September 22, 2015.

48. Michelle Raheja, "Visual Sovereignty," in *Native Studies Keywords*, ed. Stephanie Nohelani Teves, Andrea Smith, and Michelle Raheja (Tucson: University of Arizona Press, 2015), 28.

49. Ibid.

50. Shana Redmond, *Anthem: Social Movements and the Sound of Solidarity in the African Diaspora* (New York: New York University Press, 2014), 1.

51. Patrick Wolfe, "Settler Colonialism and the Elimination of the Native," *Journal of Genocide Research* 8, no. 4 (December 2006): 388.

52. Glen Coulthard, *Red Skin, White Masks: Rejecting the Colonial Politics of Recognition* (Minneapolis: University of Minnesota Press, 2014), 3.

53. Ibid., 7.

54. Byrd, *The Transit of Empire*, xiii.

55. Ibid., 63.

56. Coulthard, *Red Skin, White Masks*, 48.

57. Audra Simpson, *Mohawk Interrupts: Political Life Across the Borders of Settler States.* (Durham, NC: Duke University Press, 2014), 33.

58. Ibid.

Chapter One

1. Scott Richard Lyons, "Actually Existing Indian Nations: Modernity, Diversity, and the Future of Native American Studies," *American Indian Quarterly* 35, no. 3 (Summer 2011): 305.

2. Frantz Fanon, *The Wretched of the Earth* (New York: Grove Press, 2004), 3.

3. Lyons, "Actually Existing Indian Nations," 305.

4. Scott Richard Lyons, "There's No Translation for It: The Rhetorical Sovereignty of Indigenous Languages," in *Cross-Language Relations in Composition*, ed. Bruce Horner, Min-Zhan Lu, and Paul Matsuda (Carbondale: Southern Illinois University Press, 2010), 127–41. Lyons makes a great point about this throughout the essay, but he does it in a way that would not render Native communities in limited ways.

5. J. Ivy, *Dear Father: Breaking the Cycle of Pain* (New York: Atria Books, 2015), xvi.

6. I do want to give a shout out to War Party, who has been around for some time in Canada. Karyn Recollet's dissertation does a fantastic job with that history.

7. Alan Aquallo, "Without Reservations: Native Hip Hop and Identity in the Music of W.O.R." (University of San Diego, 2009), 56.

8. Paul Caat Smith and Robert A. Warrior, *Like A Hurricane: American Indian Activism from Alcatraz to Wounded Knee* (Boston: The Free Press, 1995).

9. For a general overview see Paul Chaat Smith and Robert A. Warrior, *Like a Hurricane* (Boston: South End Press, 1995). For a focus specific to Native women see Donna Langston, "American Indian Women's Activism in the 1960s and 1970s," *Hypatia* 18, no. 2, special issue: Indigenous Women in the Americas (spring, 2003). At least two authors depart from the belief that Native activism began with AIM. See Daniel Cobb and Loretta Fowler, eds., *Beyond Red Power: American Indian Politics and Activism Since 1900.* (Santa Fe: School for Advanced Research Press, 2007) and Bradley G. Shreve, *Red Power Rising: The National Indian Youth Council and the Origins of Native Activism* (Norman: University of Oklahoma Press, 2011). I would agree with Shreve that the roots of red power go back at least since 1961, but the high points of activism occurred between the years 1968 and 1976. For critical memoirs of the American Indian movement see Dennis Banks with Richard Erodes, *Ojibwa Warrior: Dennis Banks and the Rise of the American Indian Movement* (Norman: University of Oklahoma Press, 2004) and Russell Means's *Where White Men Fear to Tread: The Autobiography of Russell Means* (New York: St. Martin's Press, 1995).

10. Stephen Cornell, *The Return of the Native: American Indian Political Resurgence* (Cambridge: Oxford University Press, 1988).

11. For discussions of neoliberalism, see David Harvey, *A Brief History of Neoliberalism* (Cambridge: Oxford University Press, 2007); Joseph Stiglitz, *Globalization and Its Discontents* (New York: W. W. Norton & Co., 2002).

12. http://indiancountrytodaymedianetwork.com/2013/02/28/calif ornia-educator-bridges-generation-gap-hip-hop-147707. Accessed November 10, 2015.

13. Maureen T. Schwarz, *Fighting Colonialism with Hegemonic Culture: Native American Appropriation of Indian Stereotypes* (Albany: State University of New York Press, 2013). Schwarz contends that Native people today manipulate colonial images for their own purposes.

14. Kate Jorgensen and Melissa Leal, *Rebel Music: Native America. Teacher's Guide*, 1. Context Lesson Plan and Episode Discussion Guide. https://legacy.wlu.ca/documents/59892/RebelED_NativeAmerica_ LessonPlan.pdf. Accessed June 21, 2015.

15. David Macdonald and Daniel Wilson, "Poverty or Prosperity: Indigenous Children in Canada," 16. Canadian Centre for Policy Alternatives, June 2013. https://www.policyalternatives.ca/sites/default/files/uploads/publications/National%20Office/2013/06/Poverty_or_Prosperity_Indigenous_Children.pdf.

16. http://rpm.fm/artist/q-rock/. Accessed April 4, 2016.

17. Christian Parrish Takes the Gun, "Supaman: Rapping on the Reservation," October 10, 2011, http://www.npr.org/2011/10/11/141238763/supaman-rapping-on-the-reservation.

18. http://www.powwows.com/2014/02/21/prayer-song-loop-by-supaman/. Accessed November 15, 2015.

19. Monica R. Miller, *Religion and Hip Hop.* (New York: Routledge, 2012). Ebony Utley, *Rap and Religion: Understanding the Gangsta's God.* (Santa Barbara, CA: ABC-CLIO, 2012); Monica R. Miller, Anthony B. Pinn, and Bernard "Bun B" Freeman, eds., *Religion in Hip Hop: Mapping the New Terrain in the US* (Bloomsbury Academic: London and New York, 2015).

20. Eduardo Bonilla-Silva, *Racism Without Racists: Color-Blind Racism and the Persistence of Racial Inequality in the United States* (New York: Rowman & Littlefield Publishers, Inc., 2003).

21. Scott Richard Lyons, *X-Marks: Native Signatures of Assent* (Minneapolis: University of Minnesota Press, 2010), 60.

22. Russell Means and Marvin J. Wolf, *Where White Fear to Tread: The Autobiography of Russell Means* (New York: St. Martin's Griffin, 1996), 153.

23. Ibid.

24. Nataanii Means, "The Radical," 2 *Worlds*. 2013.

25. https://www.youtube.com/watch?v=pW7cLgozECc. Accessed December 29, 2015.

26. For a fuller discussion see, Geneva Smitherman's *Talkin and Testifyin: The Language of Black America* (1986), especially chapter five titled, "The Forms of Things Unknown: Black Modes of Discourse," 101–66. Geneva Smitherman; specifically to hip hop, check out Geneva Smitherman, "The Chain Remain the Same: Communicative Practices in the Hip Hop Nation," *The Black Scholar* 28, no. 1 (1997): 3–25; see also H. Samy Alim, *Roc the Mic: The Language of Hip Hop Culture* (New York and London: Routledge, 2006).

27. *Talkin and Testifyin*, 118–19.

28. Ibid., 121.

29. https://frankwaln47.bandcamp.com/track/what-makes-the-red-man-red. Accessed December 28, 2015.

30. James Baldwin, *The Fire Next Time* (New York: Vintage International, 1993), 95.

Chapter Two

1. Elena Romero, *Free Stylin': How Hip Hop Changed the Fashion Industry* (Santa Barbara, CA: Praeger, 2012), 9.

2. Robert Berkhofer, Jr., *The White Man's Indian: Images of the American Indian from Columbus to the Present* (New York: Vintage Books, 1978), 76.

3. Ibid.

4. Jessica Metcalfe, "Native Designers of High Fashion: Expressing Identity, Creativity, and Tradition in Contemporary Customary Clothing." Dissertation, University of Arizona, 2010, 337.

5. Ibid., 355.

6. Chase Manhattan, "How I Feel." *Warrior DNA.* (2015).

7. https://www.ephin.com/collections/drezus/products/air-drezus-sticker?variant=14760970246. Accessed January 11, 2017.

8. SouFy, interview with the author, September 11, 2016.

9. Ibid.

10. David E. Kirkland, "The Skin We Ink: Tattoos, Literacy, and a New English Education," *English Education* 41, no. 4: 389.

11. Ernie Paniccioli, *Who Shot Ya? Three Decades of Hip Hop Photography*, ed. Kevin Powell (New York: Harper Collins Publishing, 2002).

12. Ibid., 177–79.

Chapter Three

1. Laura Tohoe, "There Is No Word for Feminism in My Language," *Wicazo Sa Review* 15, no. 2 (Autumn 2000): 103–10.

2. Maile Arvin, Eve Tuck, and Angie Morrill, "Decolonizing Feminism: Challenging Connection Between Settler Colonialism and Heteropatriarchy," *Feminist Formations* 25, no. 1 (Spring 2013): 11.

3. Ibid., 10.

4. Judy told me this during an interview we did in June 2014. For a brief history of DRUM, see Dan Georgakas and Marvin Surkin, *Detroit: I Do Mind Dying: A Study in Urban Revolution* (New York: St. Martin's Press, 1975).

5. Renya Ramirez, "Learning Across Differences: Native and Ethnic Studies Feminisms," *American Quarterly* 60, no. 2 (June 2008): 303.

6. Tricia Rose, *The Hip Hop Wars: What We Talk About When We Talk About Hip Hop—and Why It Matters* (New York: Basic Civitas Books, 2008); Gwendolyn Pough, *Check It While I Wreck It: Black Womanhood, Hip-Hop Culture, and the Public Sphere* (Boston: Northeastern University Press, 2004); Ruth Nicole Brown and Chamara J. Kwakye, *Wish to Live: The Hip-hop Feminism Pedagogy Reader* (New York: Peter Lang Publishing, 2012).

7. Gwendolyn Pough, Elaine Richardson, Aisha Durham, and Rachel Raimist, eds., *Home Girls Make Some Noise!: Hip-Hop Feminism Anthology* (Mira Loma, CA: Parker Publishing, LLC), 2007; Joan Morgan, *When Chickenheads Come Home to Roost: A Hip-Hop Feminist Breaks it Down* (New York: Simon & Schuster, 2000); Aisha Durham, *Home With Hip Hop Feminism: Performances in Communication and Culture* (New York: Peter Lang, 2014); Elaine Richardson, " 'She was workin like foreal': Critical Literacy and Discourse practices of African American females in the age of Hip Hop," *Discourse and Society* 18, no. 6: 789–809.

8. Byron Hurt, *Hip-Hop: Beyond Beats and Rhymes*, Full Screen, Color, NTSC, DVD (Media Education Foundation, 2006).

9. Victor Rios, *Punished: Policing the Lives of Black and Latino Boys* (New York: New York University Press, 2011).

10. Aimé Ellis, *If We Must Die: From Bigger Thomas to Biggie Smalls* (Detroit: Wayne State University Press, 2011), 4.

11. Michelle Alexander, *The New Jim Crow: Mass Incarceration in an Age of Colorblindness* (New York: The Free Press, 2010).

12. Ibid., 17.

13. bell hooks, *We Real Cool: Black Men and Masculinity* (New York: Routledge, 2004), xii.

14. Kyle T. Mays, *The Indigenous Motor City: Indigenous People and the Making of Modern Detroit* (in progress, under contract with the University of Washington Press).

15. Coulthard, *Red Skin, White Masks*, 178.

16. Ellis, *If We Must Die: From Bigger Thomas to Biggie Smalls*; hooks, *We Real Cool: Black Men and Masculinity*; David Kirkland, *A Search Past Silence: The Literacy of Young Black Men* (New York: Teachers College Press, 2013); Richard Majors and Janet Billson, *Cool Pose: The Dilemmas of Black Manhood in America* (New York: Macmillan, Inc., 1992). David E. Kirkland and Austin Jackson, " 'We Real Cool': Toward a Theory of Black Masculine Literacies," *Reading Research Quarterly* 44, no. 3 (July 2009): 278–97.

17. Timothy J. Brown, "Welcome to the Terrordome: Exploring the Contradictions of a Hip-Hop Black Masculinity," in *Progressive Black Masculinities*, ed. Athena Mutua (New York: Routledge, 2006), 207.

18. Ty P. Kawika Tengan, *Native Men Remade: Gender and Nation in Contemporary Hawai'i* (Durham, NC: Duke University Press, 2008).

19. Sam McKegney, "Into the Full Grace of the Blood of Men: An Introduction by Sam McKegney," in *Masculindians: Conversations About Indigenous Manhood*, ed. Sam McKegney (Winnipeg: University of Manitoba Press, 2014), 5.

20. Maureen T. Schwarz, *Fighting Colonialism with Hegemonic Culture: Native American Appropriation of Indian Stereotypes* (Albany: State University of New York Press, 2013), 3.

21. Frank Waln, "My Stone."

22. XXL Staff, "2Pac's "Dear Mama" inducted into Library of Congress Registry." June 24, 2010. http://www.xxlmag.com/xxl-magazine/2010/06/tupacs-dear-mama-inducted-into-library-of-congress-registry/.

23. Leanne Simpson, *Islands of Decolonial Love: Stories and Songs* (Winnipeg, Manitoba: ARP Books, 2013), 85.

24. Robert Alexander Innes, "Moose on the Loose: Indigenous Men, Violence, and the Colonial Excuse (with Errata)," *Aboriginal Policy Studies* 4, no. 1 (2015): 51.

25. hooks, *Black Men and Masculinity*, 159.

26. Ibid.

27. https://www.youtube.com/watch?v=VA3uRLZ_1zM. Accessed December 15, 2015.

28. Durham, *Home With Hip Hop* Feminism, 3.

29. Maile Arvin, Eve Tuck, and Angie Morrill, "Decolonizing Feminism: Challenging Connection Between Settler Colonialism and Heteropatriarchy," *Feminist Formations* 25, no. 1 (Spring 2013): 8–34.

30. Eekwol, "I will not be conquered." *Good Kill.* Produced by Merky Waters. 2015.

31. Kim Anderson, "Affirmation of an Indigenous Feminist," in *Indigenous Women and Feminism: Politics, Activism, Culture* (Vancouver: University of British Columbia Press, 2010), 89.

32. http://www.cbc.ca/news/canada/manitoba/the-life-of-wab-ki new-from-rapper-and-broadcaster-to-author-and-candidate-1.3489489. Accessed March 14, 2016.

33. http://www.cbc.ca/news/canada/manitoba/manitoba-liberals-wab-k inew-misogynistic-comments-1.3487073. Accessed March 14, 2016.

34. Wab Kinew, *The Reason You Walk: A Memoir* (Toronto, CA: Penguin Random House, 2015), 272.

35. Leanne Simpson, "Not Murdered and Not Missing: Rebelling Against Colonial Gender Violence," in *Taking Sides: Revolutionary Solidarity and the Poverty of Liberalism*, ed. Cindy Milstein (Edinburgh, UK and Oakland, CA: AK Press, 2015), 117.

36. Ibid.

Chapter Four

1. David Muhammad, "Litefoot: Outkast, Stereotypes, Native America," February 27, 2004. http://allhiphop.com/2004/02/27/lite foot-outkast-stereotypes-native-america/.

2. Derrick Bell, *Faces at the Bottom of the Well: The Permanence of Racism* (New York: Basic Books, 1993); Kimberlee Crenshaw, Neil Gotanda, Gary Peller et al., eds., *Critical Race Theory: The Key Writings that Formed the Movement* (New York: The New Press, 1996).

3. Michael Omi and Howard Winant, *Racial Formation in the United States: From the 1960s to the 1990s* (New York: Routledge, 1994).

4. Joe Feagin and Sean Elias, "Rethinking Racial Formation Theory: A Systematic Racism Critique," *Ethnic and Racial Studies, Symposium on Rethinking Racial Formation Theory* 36, no. 6 (April 2012): 931–60.

5. Patricia Hill Collins and Sirma Bilge, *Intersectionality (Key Concepts),* (Cambridge, UK: Polity Press, 2016); Patricia Hill Collins, *Black Feminist Thought: Knowledge, Consciousness, and the Politics of Empowerment* (New York: Routledge, 2000).

6. Eduardo Bonilla-Silva, *Racism without Racists: Color-Blind Racism and the Persistence of Racial Inequality in the United States,* 2nd ed. (Lanham, MD: Rowman & Littlefield Publishers, Inc., 2006).

7. Byrd, *The Transit of Empire*; Glen Coulthard, *Red Skin, White Masks*; Simpson, *Mohawk Interrupts*; Patrick Wolfe, "Land, Labor, and Difference: Elementary Structures of Race," *The American Historical Review* 106, no. 3 (June 2001): 866–905.

8. Kyle T. Mays, "Transnational Progressivism: African Americans, Native Americans, and the Universal Races Congress of 1911," *American Indian Quarterly* 37, no. 3 (Summer 2013): 243–61.

9. Stephanie Fryberg et al., "Of Warrior Chiefs and Indian Princesses: The Psychological Consequences of American Indian Mascots," *Basic and Applied Social Psychology* 30 (2008): 208–18.

10. I use this term to describe how different oppressed groups compare their experiences in order to determine who has it worse given a particular issue.

11. Jay Z. *Decoded* (New York: Spiegel & Grau, 2010), 75.

12. Ibid., 86.

13. Kyle T. Mays, *Reading Indigeneity into The Rhetoric and Words of El Hajj Malik El Shabbaz: Malcolm X* (unpublished essay).

14. Ellis, *If We Must Die: From Bigger Thomas to Biggie Smalls*, 11.

15. Michelle Raheja, *Reservation Reelism: Redfacing, Visual Sovereignty, and Representations of Native Americans in Film* (Lincoln: University of Nebraska Press, 2010), 11.

16. Chief, "Blowed (feat. Snoop Dogg), *Smoke Signals EP* (2013).

17. Lisa Brooks, *The Common Pot: The Recovery of Native Space in the Northeast*, Indigenous Americas (Minneapolis: University of Minnesota Press, 2008).

18. http://www.rollingstone.com/music/news/pharrell-apologiz es-for-wearing-headdress-on-magazine-cover-20140605. Accessed November 5, 2015.

19. Geneva Smitherman, "The Chain Remain the Same: Communicative Practices in the Hip Hop Nation," *The Black Scholar* 28, no. 1 (1997): 11.

20. *Rebel Music: Native America*. Documentary. November 2014. https:// www.youtube.com/watch?v=-aRwprNai4A.

21. For a recent, whole volume dedicated to black language, see Sonja Lanehart, ed., *The Oxford Handbook of African American Language* (New York: Oxford University Press, 2015).

22. Smitherman, *Talkin and Testifyin: The Language of Black America*, 2.

23. Geneva Smitherman, "'A New Way of Talkin': Language, Social Change, and Political Theory," in *Talkin That Talk: Language, Culture, and Education in African America* (New York: Routledge, 1999), 94.

24. Ibid.

25. Fanon, *Black Skin, White Masks*, 1–2.

26. Alim, *Roc the Mic: The Language of Hip Hop Culture*.

27. Geneva Smitherman, "The Chain Remain the Same: Communicative Practices in the Hip Hop Nation," *The Black Scholar* 28, no. 1 (1997): 11.

28. Problems Facing Native American Youths. United States Senate, 107 Congress (2003).

29. Daryl Baldwin and Julie Olds, "Miami Indian Language and Cultural Research at Miami University," in *Beyond Red Power: New Perspectives on American Indian Politics and Activism*, ed. Daniel Cobb and Loretta Fowler, 280–90. Santa Fe: School of Advanced Research, 2007.

30. Eva Marie Garroutte and Kathleen Delores Westcott, "The Story Is a Living Being: Companionship with Stories in Anishinaabeg Studies,"

in *Centering Anishinaabeg Studies: Understanding the World through Stories*, ed. Jill Doerfler, Niigaanwewidam James Sinclair, and Heidi Kiiwetinepinesiik Stark (East Lansing: Michigan State University Press, 2013), 70.

31. John Reyner and Jeanne Eder, *American Indian Education: A History* (Norman: University of Oklahoma Press, 2006); Brenda Childs, *Boarding School Seasons: American Indian Families, 1900–1940* (Lincoln: University of Nebraska Press, 2000); Doug Adams, *Education for Extinction: American Indians and the Boarding School Experience* (Lawrence: University of Kansa Press, 1995); Andrew Woolford, *This Benevolent Experiment: Indigenous Boarding Schools, Genocide, and Redress in Canada and the United States* (Winnipeg: University of Manitoba Press, 2015).

32. Dylan A. T. Miner, "Stories as Mshkiki: Reflections on the Healing and Migratory Practices of Minwaajimo," in *Centering Anishinaabeg Studies: Understanding the World Through Stories*, ed. Jill Doerfler, Niigaanwediam James Sinclair, and Heidi Stark (East Lansing: Michigan State University Press, 2013), 319.

33. Lee Maracle, *Oratory: Coming to Theory* (Vancouver: Gallerie Publications, 1990), 3.

34. Scott Richard Lyons, "There's No Translation for It: The Rhetorical Sovereignty of Indigenous Languages," in *Cross-Language Relations in Composition*, ed. B. Homer, MZ. Lu and P. Matsusada (Southern Illinois University Press: Carbondale, 2010), 139.

35. Ibid.

36. http://blacklivesmatter.com/herstory/. Accessed July 25, 2016.

37. http://www.npr.org/sections/thetwo-way/2015/12/28/461293703/grand-jury-declines-to-indict-police-officers-in-tamir-rice-investigation. Accessed December 28, 2015.

38. Derrick A. Bell, Jr., "Brown v. Board of Education and the Interest Convergence Dilemma," *Harvard Law Review* 93, no. 518 (1980): 524.

39. For another example, see Leanne Simpson, "Indict the System: Indigenous and Black Connected Resistance," *Leanne Betasamosake Simpson*, November 28, 2014, http://leannesimpson.ca/indict-the-system-indigenous-black-connected-resistance/.

40. Chadwick Allen, *Trans-Indigenous: Methodologies for Global Native Literary Studies* (Minneapolis: University of Minnesota Press, 2012).

41. http://www.nytimes.com/2014/12/18/us/judge-vacates-conviction-in-1944-execution.html?_r=0. Accessed December 28, 2015.

42. Claudia Rankine, *Citizen: An American Lyric* (Minneapolis: Graywolf Press, 2014),

43. Tall Paul, "No Questions," *No Good Guy* (2015). https://tallpaul612.bandcamp.com/track/no-questions-prod-by-rube.

44. Eric Heisig, "City of Cleveland to pay $6 million to Tamir Rice's family to settle lawsuit," April 25, 2016. *Cleveland.com*. http://www.cleveland.com/court-justice/index.ssf/2016/04/city_of_cleveland_to_pay_6_mil.html.

45. Krishnadev Calamur, "No Indictment in the Tamir Rice Shooting," December 28, 2015. http://www.theatlantic.com/national/archive/2015/12/tamir-rice-indictment/422049/.

46. Ryan Felton. "Flint Water Crisis: Rick Snyder's emails leave more questions than answers," https://www.theguardian.com/us-news/2016/jan/21/flint-water-crisis-michigan-governor-rick-snyder-emails-redacted.

47. http://www.colorlines.com/articles/flint-continue-receiving-detroit-water-without-price-increase. Great Lakes Water Authority has been around since January 2016. Emergency Financial Manager Kevin Orr proposed this as a part of pulling Detroit out of its debt problem. For more information about the GLWA, see http://www.glwater.org/about-us/.

48. https://soundcloud.com/soufy313/pay-to-be-poisoned-ft-zebra-octobra-lisa-brunk-prod-by-native-keyz. Accessed June 28, 2016.

49. Christina Laughlin, http://www.huffingtonpost.com/christina-laughlin/flint-is-not-the-only-one_b_9287798.html. Accessed May 24, 2016.

50. Justin Gardner, http://thefreethoughtproject.com/navajo-water-supply-horrific-flint-cares-native-american/. Accessed May 25, 2016.

51. SouFy featuring Lisa Brunk, "Pay to Be Poisoned," 2016. https://soundcloud.com/soufy313/pay-to-be-poisoned-ft-zebra-octobra-lisa-brunk-prod-by-native-keyz. Lyrics used with permission.

52. Paul Egan, "Amid denials, state workers in Flint got clean water," January 29, 2016, *Detroit Free Press*. http://www.freep.com/

story/news/local/michigan/flint-water-crisis/2016/01/28/amid-de
nials-state-workers-flint-got-clean-water/79470650/.

53. David A. Graham, "What Did the Governor Know About Flint's
Water, and When Did He Know It?," *The Atlantic*, January 9, 2016. http://
www.theatlantic.com/politics/archive/2016/01/what-did-the-governor-kn
ow-about-flints-water-and-when-did-he-know-it/423342/.

54. "Nakweshkodaadiidaa Ekoobiiyag [Let's Meet Up by the Water]
by Sacramento Knoxx featuring Christy B. Kaz Clever, 2016. https://
sknoxx.bandcamp.com/track/nakweshkodaadiidaa-ekoobiiyag-let
s-meet-up-by-the-water. Accessed May 3, 2016.

55. Kyle T. Mays, "Song 'Let's Meet By the Water' Invites Support at
Indigenous Water Ceremony in Flint," *Indian Country Today Media
Network*. April 14, 2016. http://indiancountrytodaymedianetwork.
com/2016/04/14/song-lets-meet-water-invites-support-indigenous-w
ater-ceremony-flint-164144. Accessed June 1, 2016.

56. http://nativenewsonline.net/currents/23974/.

Conclusion

1. http://www.cbc.ca/radio/unreserved/celebrating-the-two-spi
rit-community-1.3649115/hip-hop-artist-embraces-both-masculine-an
d-feminine-sides-1.3649450. Accessed July 8, 2016.

2. Chadwick Allen, *Trans-Indigenous: Methodologies for Global Native
Literary Studies* (Minneapolis: University of Minnesota Press, 2012).

3. Bakari Kitwana, *The Hip Hop Generation: Young Blacks and the Crisis
in African American Culture* (New York: Basic Civitas Books, 2002), 4.

4. Ibid., 23.

5. Fanon, *Black Skins, White Masks*, 145.

6. http://www.cbc.ca/radio/unreserved/resisting-reclaiming-an
d-reconnecting-to-culture-1.3577136/artist-reclaims-toronto-str
eets-using-ojibway-language-1.3581118.

7. Kate Rutherford, "Attawapiskat declares state of emergency over spate
of suicide attempts," *CBC News*. April 9, 2016. http://www.cbc.ca/news/
canada/sudbury/attawapiskat-suicide-first-nations-emergency-1.3528747.

8. Stephanie Woodward, "Youth Suicide Alarms Tribes," October 10, 2012. http://100r.org/2012/10/indian-youth-suicide-soars/.

9. Maria Yellow Horse Brave Heart and Lemyra DeBruyn, "The American Indian Holocaust: Healing Historical Unresolved Grief," *American Indian and Alaska Native Mental Health Research* 8, no. 2: 60–82. Accessed June 20, 2013. http://www.ucdenver.edu/academics/colleges/PublicHealth/research/centers/CAIANH/journal/Documents/Volume%208/8(2)_Yell owHorseBraveHeart_American_Indian_Holocaust_60-82.pdf.

10. See, for instance, Kyle T. Mays, "Pontiac's Ghost in the Motor City: Indigeneity and the Discursive Construction of Modern Detroit," *Middle West Review* 2, no. 2, (Spring 2016): 115–42.

11. See, for instance, John N. Low, *Imprints: The Pokagon Band of Potawatomi Indians and the City of Chicago* (East Lansing: Michigan State University Press, 2016). He demonstrates, through a variety of texts, the continuous presence of Pokagon Indians, and representations of them, in Chicago.

12. 2010 US Census and 2006 Canadian Census. And both populations in general are growing substantially. For Canadian source see, https://www.aadnc-aandc.gc.ca/eng/1100100014298/1100100014302. Accessed December 19, 2015.

13. Marc Lamont Hill, *Nobody: Casualties of America's War on the Vulnerable, from Ferguson to Flint and Beyond* (New York: Atria Books, 2016), 28.

14. Leanne Simpson, "Not Murdered and Not Missing: Rebelling Against Colonial Gender Violence," in *Taking Sides: Revolutionary Solidarity and the Poverty of Liberalism*, ed. Cindy Milstein, 114–23. Edinburgh, UK and Oakland, CA: AK Press, 2015, 120.

15. For a detailed account of Standing Rock, please see the "Standing Rock Syllabus." It serves as a thorough source of information on Standing Rock, the history of the tribe, and the problems with the Dakota Access Pipeline as it relates to Standing Rock sovereignty. https://nycstandswithstand ingrock.wordpress.com/standingrocksyllabus/.

16. Kyle T. Mays, "From Flint to Standing Rock: The Aligned Struggles of Black and Indigenous People," *Cultural Anthropology "Hot Spots,"*

December 22, 2016. https://culanth.org/fieldsights/1015-from-flint-to-sta
nding-rock-the-aligned-struggles-of-black-and-indigenous-people.

17. Joyce Green, "Taking Account of Aboriginal Feminism," in *Making Space for Indigenous Feminism*, 25 (Winnipeg: Fernwood Publishing, 2007).

18. Shari Huhndorf and Cheryl Suzack, "Indigenous Feminism: Theorizing the Issues," in *Indigenous Women and Feminism: Politics, Activism, Culture*, ed. Cheryl Suzack, Shari Huhndorf, Jeanne Perreault, and Jean Barman, 9. Vancouver, British Columbia: University of British Columbia Press, 2010.

19. http://www.hotnewhiphop.com/hip-hop-reacts-to-dakota-access-pipeline-reroute-news.25958.html?. Accessed January 11, 2017.

20. Angela Y. Davis, *Freedom is a Constant Struggle: Ferguson, Palestine, and the Foundations of a Movement*, ed. Frank Barat (Chicago: Haymarket Books, 2016), 16.

21. James Sledd, "Bi-Dialectalism: The Linguistics of White Supremacy," *English Journal* 58, no. 9 (December 1969): 1309.

22. Ibid.

23. Coulthard, *Red Skin, White Masks*, 3.

24. Nina Shapiro, http://www.seattletimes.com/seattle-news/north-west/native-lawyer-takes-on-tribes-that-kick-members-out/. Accessed December 19, 2015.

25. Jill Doerfler, *Those Who Belong: Family, Blood, and Citizenship among the White Earth Anishinaabeg* (East Lansing: Michigan State University Press, 2015).

26. Lyons, *X-Marks*, 61.

27. Watkins, *Hip Hop Matters*. He offers a chapter on this very subject.

28. Django Paris, "Culturally Sustaining Pedagogy: A Needed Change in Stance, Terminology, and Practice," *Educational Researcher* 41, no. 3 (2012): 95.

29. Teresa McCarty and Tiffany Lee, "Critical Culturally Sustaining/Revitalizing Pedagogy and Indigenous Education Sovereignty," *Harvard Educational Review* 84, no. 1 (April 2014): 103.

30. Eve Tuck and K. Wayne Yang, "Decolonization Is Not a Metaphor," *Decolonization: Indigeneity, Education and Society* 1, no. 1 (2012): 1–40.

WORKS CITED

Adams, David. *Education for Extinction: American Indians and the Boarding School Experience*. Lawrence, KS: University of Kansas Press, 1995.

Alexander, Michelle. *The New Jim Crow: Mass Incarceration in the Age of Colorblindness*. New York: The New Press, 2010.

Alim, H. Samy. "Global Ill-Literacies: Hip Hop Cultures, Youth Identities, and the Politics of Literacy." *Review of Research in Education* 35, no. 1 (March 2011): 120–46.

———. *Roc the Mic: The Language of Hip Hop Culture*. New York and London: Routledge, 2006.

Alim, H. Samy, Awad Ibrahim, and Alastair Pennycook, eds. *Global Linguistic Flows: Hip Hop Cultures, Youth Identities, and the Politics of Language*. New York: Routledge, 2009.

Allen, Chadwick. *Trans-Indigenous: Methodologies for Global Native Literary Studies*. Minneapolis: University of Minnesota Press, 2012.

Aquallo, Alan. "Without Reservations: Native Hip Hop and Identity in the Music of W.O.R." Doctoral dissertation, University of San Diego, 2009.

Arvin, Maile. "Analytics of Indigeneity." In *Native Studies Keywords*, edited by Stephanie Nohelani Teves, Andrea Smith, and Michelle Raheja, 119–29. Tucson: University of Arizona Press, 2015.

Arvin, Maile, Eve Tuck, and Angie Morrill. "Decolonizing Feminism: Challenging Connection between Settler Colonialism and Heteropatriarchy." *Feminist Formations* 25, no. 1 (Spring 2013): 8–34.

Bakhtin, Mikhail. *The Dialogic Imagination: Four Essays*. Edited by Michael Holquist. Translated by Caryl Emerson and Michael Holquist. Austin: University of Texas Press, 1981.

Baldwin, Daryl, and Julie Olds. "Miami Indian Language and Cultural Research at Miami University." In *Beyond Red Power: New Perspectives on American Indian Politics and Activism*, edited by Daniel Cobb and

Loretta Fowler, 280–90. Santa Fe, NM: School of Advanced Research, 2007.

Baldwin, James. *The Fire Next Time*. New York: Vintage International, 1993.

Banks, Dennis. *Ojibwa Warrior: Dennis Banks and the Rise of the American Indian Movement*. Edited by Richard Erodes. Norman: University of Oklahoma Press, 2004.

Bell, Derrick. *Faces at the Bottom of the Well: The Permanence of Racism*. New York: Basic Books, 1993.

Bell, Jr., Derrick A. "Brown v. Board of Education and the Interest Convergence Dilemma." *Harvard Law Review* 93, no. 518 (1980): 518–33.

Berglund, Jeff, Jan Johnson, and Kimberli Lee, eds. "Introduction." In *Indigenous Pop: Native American Music from Jazz to Hip Hop*, 3–16. Tucson: University of Arizona Press, 2016.

Berkhofer, Jr., Robert. *The White Man's Indian: Images of the American Indian from Columbus to the Present*. New York: Vintage Press, 1979.

Bonilla-Silva, Eduardo. *Racism without Racists: Color-Blind Racism and the Persistence of Racial Inequality in the United States*. Lahman, MD: Rowman & Littlefield Publishers, 2006.

Boyd, Colleen, and Coll Thrush, eds. *Phantom Past, Indigenous Presence: Native Ghosts in North American Culture and History*. Lincoln: University of Nebraska Press, 2011.

Brooks, Lisa. *The Common Pot: The Recovery of Native Space in the Northeast*. Indigenous Americas. Minneapolis: University of Minnesota Press, 2008.

Brown, Ruth Nicole, and Chamara Kwakye, eds. *Wish to Live: The Hip Hop Feminism Pedagogy Reader*. New York: Peter Lang, 2012.

Brown, Timothy J., and Athena Mutua. "Welcome to the Terrordome: Exploring the Contradictions of a Hip-Hop Black Masculinity." In *Progressive Black Masculinities*. New York: Routledge, 2006.

Byrd, Jodi. *The Transit of Empire: Indigenous Critiques of Colonialism*. Minneapolis: University of Minnesota Press, 2011.

Chang, Jeff. *Can't Stop, Won't Stop: A History of the Hip Hop Generation*. New York: St. Martin's Press, 2005.

———. "It's a Hip-Hop World." *Foreign Policy*, December 2007.

Collins, Patricia Hill. *Black Feminist Thought: Knowledge, Consciousness, and the Politics of Empowerment*. New York: Routledge, 2000.

Collins, Patricia Hill, and Sirma Bilge. *Intersectionality (Key Concepts)*. Cambridge, UK: Polity, 2016.

Cornell, Stephen. *The Return of the Native: American Indian Political Resurgence*. Cambridge, UK: Oxford University Press, 1988.

Coulthard, Glen. *Red Skin, White Masks: Rejecting the Colonial Politics of Recognition*. Minneapolis: University of Minnesota Press, 2014.

Crenshaw, Kimberlee, Neil Gotanda, and Gary Peller, eds. *Critical Race Theory: The Key Writings That Formed the Movement*. New York: The New Press, 1996.

Davis, Angela Y. *Freedom Is A Constant Struggle: Ferguson, Palestine, and the Foundations of a Movement*. Edited by Frank Barat. Chicago: Haymarket Books, 2016.

Deloria, Philip. *Indians in Unexpected Places*. Lawrence, KS: University Press of Kansas, 2004.

———. *Playing Indian*. New Haven and London: Yale University Press, 1998.

Demallie, Raymond J. "The Lakota Ghost Dance: An Ethnohistorical Account." *Pacific Historical Review* 51, no. 4 (1982): 385–405.

Doerfler, Jill. *Those Who Belong: Family, Blood, and Citizenship among the White Earth Anishinaabeg*. East Lansing: Michigan State University, 2015.

Durham, Aisha S. *Home With Hip Hop Feminism: Performances in Communication and Culture*. Vol. 26. Intersections in Communications and Cultures. New York: Peter Lang, 2014.

Ellis, Aimé. *If We Must Die: From Bigger Thomas to Biggie Smalls*. Detroit: Wayne State University Press, 2011.

Fanon, Frantz. *Black Skin, White Masks*. New York: Grove Press, 2008.

———. *The Wretched of the Earth*. New York: Grove Press, 2004.

Feagin, Joe, and Sean Elias. "Rethinking Racial Formation Theory: A Systematic Racism Critique." *Ethnic and Racial Studies*, Symposium on Rethinking Racial Formation Theory 36, no. 6 (April 2012): 931–60.

Fernandes, Sujatha. *Close to the Edge: In Search of the Global Hip Hop Generation*. London and Brooklyn: Verso, 2011.

Fixico, Donald. *Termination and Relocation: Federal Indian Policy, 1945–1960*. Albuquerque: University of New Mexico Press, 1986.

——. *The Urban Indian Experience in America*. Albuquerque: University of New Mexico Press, 2000.

Fowler, Loretta. *Beyond Red Power: American Indian Politics and Activism Since 1900*. Edited by Daniel Cobb. Santa Fe: School for Advanced Research, 2007.

Fryberg, Stephanie, Hazel Rose Markus, Daphna Oyserman, and Joseph Stone. "Of Warrior Chiefs and Indian Princesses: The Psychological Consequences of American Indian Mascots." *Basic and Applied Social Psychology* 30 (2008): 208–18.

Garroutte, Eva Marie, and Kathleen Delores Westcott. "The Story Is a Living Being: Companionship with Stories in Anishinaabeg Studies." In *Centering Anishinaabeg Studies: Understanding the World through Stories*, edited by Jill Doerfler, Niigaanwewidam James Sinclair, and Heidi Kiiwetinepinesiik Stark, 61–80. East Lansing: Michigan State University Press, 2013.

Georgakas, Dan, and Marvin Surkin. *Detroit: I Do Mind Dying: A Study in Urban Revolution*. New York: St. Martin's Press, 1975.

Gilroy, Paul. *The Black Atlantic: Modernity and Double Consciousness*. Cambridge: Harvard University Press, 1993.

Harvey, David. *A Brief History of Neoliberalism*. Cambridge: Oxford University Press, 2007.

Hill, Marc Lamont. *Nobody: Casualties of America's War on the Vulnerable, from Ferguson to Flint and Beyond*. New York: Atria Books, 2016.

Holland, Sharon P., and Tiya Miles. "Afro-Native Realities." In *The World of Indigenous North America*, edited by Robert Warrior, 524–48. New York: Routledge, 2015.

hooks, bell. *We Real Cool: Black Men and Masculinity*. New York: Routledge, 2004.

Ignace, Marianne. " 'Why Is My People Sleeping': First Nations Hip Hop between the Rez and the City." In *Aboriginal Peoples in Canadian*

Cities: Transformations and Continuities, edited by Heather Howard and Craig Proulx, 203–26. Waterloo, Ontario: Wilfrid Laurier University Press, 2011.

Innes, Robert Alexander. "Moose on the Loose: Indigenous Men, Violence, and the Colonial Excuse (with Errata)." *Aboriginal Policy Studies* 4, no. 1 (2015): 46–56.

Ivy, J. *Breaking the Cycle of Pain*. New York: Atria Books, 2015.

Jay Z. *Decoded*. New York: Spiegel & Grau, 2010.

Kirkland, David. *A Search Past Silence: The Literacy of Young Black Men*. New York: Teachers College Press, 2013.

Kirkland, David E. "The Skin We Ink: Tattoos, Literacy, and a New English Education." *English Education* 41, no. 4 (July 2009): 375–95.

Kirkland, David E., and Austin Jackson. " 'We Real Cool': Toward A Theory of Black Masculine Literacies." *Reading Research Quarterly* 44, no. 3 (July 2009): 278–97.

Kitwana, Bakari. *The Hip Hop Generation: Young Blacks and the Crisis in African American Culture*. New York: Basic Civitas Books, 2002.

Langston, Donna. "American Indian Women's Activism in the 1960s and 1970s." *Hypatia* 18, no. 2 (Spring 2003): 114–32.

Lashua, Bret, and Karen Fox. " 'Rec Needs a New Rhythm Cuz Rap Is Where I'm Livin'." *Leisure Sciences* 28 (2006): 268–83.

Low, John N. *Imprints: The Pokagon Band of Potawatomi Indians and the City of Chicago*. East Lansing: Michigan State University Press, 2016.

Lyons, Scott Richard. "Actually Existing Indian Nations: Modernity, Diversity, and the Future of Native American Studies." *American Indian Quarterly* 35, no. 3 (Summer 2011): 294–312.

——. "There's No Translation for It: The Rhetorical Sovereignty of Indigenous Languages." In *Cross-Language Relations in Composition*, edited by Bruce Horner, Min-Zhan Lu, and Paul Matsuda, 127–41. Carbondale: Southern Illinois University Press, 2010.

——. *X-Marks: Native Signatures of Assent*. Minneapolis: University of Minnesota Press, 2010.

Mackay, Gail. "A Reading of Eekwol's Apprentice to the Mystery as an Expression of Cree Youth's Cultural Role and Responsibility."

In *Indigenous Pop: Native American Music from Jazz to Hip Hop*, 201–23. Tucson: University of Arizona Press, 2016.

Majors, Richard, and Janet Billson. *Cool Pose: The Dilemmas of Black Manhood in America*. New York: Macmillan, Inc., 1992.

Marable, Manning. "Blackness Beyond Boundaries: Navigating the Political Economies of Global Inequality." In *Transnational Blackness: Navigating the Global Color Line*, edited by Manning Marable and Vanessa Agard-Jones, 1–8. New York: Palgrave Macmillan, 2008.

Marable, Manning, and Vanessa Agard-Jones, eds. *Transnational Blackness: Navigating the Global Color Line*. New York: Palgrave-Macmillan, 2008.

Maracle, Lee. *Oratory: Coming to Theory*. Gallerie: Women Artists' Monographs. Vancouver, British Columbia: Gallerie Publications, 1990.

Mays, Kyle T. "Indigenous Detroit: Indigeneity, Modernity, and Racial and Gender Formation in a Modern American City, 1871–2000." Doctoral dissertation, University of Illinois, Urbana-Champaign, 2015.

———. "Pontiac's Ghost in the Motor City: Indigeneity and the Discursive Construction of Modern Detroit." *The Middle West Review* 2, no. 2 (Spring 2016): 115–42.

———. "Promoting Sovereignty, Rapping Mshkiki (Medicine): A Critical (Anishinaabeg) Reading of Rapper Tall Paul's 'Prayers in a Song.'" *Social Identities: Journal for the Study of Race, Nation and Culture* 22, no. 2 (February 2016): 195–209. doi:10.1080/13504630.2015.1121574.

———. "Transnational Progressivism: African Americans, Native Americans, and the Universal Races Congress of 1911." *American Indian Quarterly* 37, no. 3 (Summer 2013): 243–61.

McCarty, Teresa, and Tiffany Lee. "Critical Culturally Sustaining/ Revitalizing Pedagogy and Indigenous Education Sovereignty." *Harvard Educational Review* 84, no. 1 (April 2014): 101–24.

McKegney, Sam. "Into the Full Grace of the Blood of Men: An Introduction by Sam McKegney." In *Masculindians: Conversations About Indigenous Manhood*, edited by Sam McKegney, 1–13. Winnipeg: University of Manitoba Press, 2014.

Means, Russell, and Marvin J. Wolf. *Where White Fear to Tread: The Autobiography of Russell Means*. New York: St. Martin's Griffin, 1996.

Metcalfe, Jessica. "Native Designers of High Fashion: Expressing Identity, Creativity, and Tradition in Contemporary Customary Clothing." Doctoral dissertation, University of Arizona, 2010.

Miller, Monica. *Religion and Hip Hop*. New York: Routledge, 2012.

Miller, Monica R., Anthony B. Pinn, and Bernard (Bun B) Freeman, eds. *Religion in Hip Hop: Mapping the New Terrain in the US*. London and New York: Bloomsbury Academic, 2015.

Miner, Dylan A.T. "Stories as Mshkiki: Reflections on the Healing and Migratory Practices of Minwaajimo." In *Centering Anishinaabeg Studies: Understanding the World through Stories*, edited by Jill Doerfler, Niigaanwewidam James Sinclair, and Heidi Kiiwetinepinesiik Stark, 317–39. East Lansing: Michigan State University Press, 2013.

Mitchell, Tony. "Blackfellas, Rapping, Breaking and Writing: A Short History of Aboriginal Rap." *Aboriginal History* 30 (2006): 124–37.

———. *Global Noise: Rap and Hip Hop Outside of the USA*. Middletown, CT: Wesleyan University Press, 2002.

Morgan, George, and Andrew Warren. "Aboriginal Youth, Hip Hop, and the Politics of Identification." *Ethnic and Racial Studies* 34, no. 6 (2010): 925–47.

Morgan, Joan. *When Chickenheads Come Home to Roost: A Hip-Hop Feminist Breaks It Down*. New York: Simon & Schuster, 2000.

Neal, Mark Anthony. *Soul Babies: Black Popular Culture and the Post-Soul Aesthetic*. New York: Routledge, 2002.

O'Brien, Jean. *Firsting and Lasting: Writing Indians Out of Existence in New England*. Minneapolis: University of Minnesota Press, 2010.

Omi, Michael, and Howard Winant. *Racial Formation in the United States: From the 1960s to the 1990s*. New York: Routledge, 1994.

Paniccioli, Ernie. *Who Shot Ya? Three Decades of Hip Hop Photography*. Edited by Kevin Powell. New York: HarperCollins Publishing, 2002.

Paris, Django. "Culturally Sustaining Pedagogy: A Needed Change in Stance, Terminology, and Practice." *Educational Researcher* 41, no. 3 (2012): 93–97.

Pough, Gwendolyn. *Check It While I Wreck It: Black Womanhood, Hip-Hop Culture, and the Public Sphere.* Boston: Northeastern University Press, 2004.

Pough, Gwendolyn, Elaine Richardson, Aisha Durham, and Rachel Raimist, eds. *Home Girls Make Some Noise!: Hip-Hop Feminism Anthology.* Mira Loma, CA: Parker Publishing LLC, 2007.

Rader, Dean. *Engaged Resistance: American Indian Art, Literature, and Film from Alcatraz to the NMAI.* Austin: University of Texas Press, 2011.

Raheja, Michelle. *Reservation Reelism: Redfacing, Visual Sovereignty, and Representations of Native Americans in Film.* Lincoln: University of Nebraska Press, 2010.

——. "Visual Sovereignty." In *Native Studies Keywords*, edited by Stephanie Nohelani Teves, 25–34. Tucson: University of Arizona Press, 2015.

Ramirez, Renya. "Learning Across Differences: Native and Ethnic Studies Feminisms." *American Quarterly* 60, no. 2 (June 2008): 303–7.

Rankine, Claudia. *Citizen: An American Lyric.* Minnesota: Graywolf Press, 2014.

Recollet, Karen. "Aural Traditions." Doctoral dissertation, Trent University, 2010.

Redmond, Shana. *Anthem: Social Movements and the Sound of Solidarity in the African Diaspora.* New York: New York University Press, 2014.

Reyner, Jon, and Jeanne Eder. *American Indian Education: A History.* Norman: University of Oklahoma Press, 2006.

Rios, Victor. *Punished: Policing the Lives of Black and Latino Boys.* New York: New York University Press, 2011.

Rivera, Raquel. *New York Ricans From the Hip Hop Zone.* New York: Palgrave-Macmillan, 2003.

Romero, Elena. *Free Stylin': How Hip Hop Changed the Fashion Industry.* Santa Barbara, CA: Praeger, 2012.

Rose, Tricia. *Black Noise: Rap Music and Black Culture in Contemporary America*. Middletown, CT: Wesleyan University Press, 1994.

———. *The Hip Hop Wars: What We Talk About When We Talk About Hip Hop—and Why It Matters*. New York: Basic Civitas Books, 2008.

Rosenthal, Nicholas. *Reimagining Indian Country: Native Migration and Identity in Twentieth Century Los Angeles*. Chapel Hill: University of North Carolina Press, 2012.

Schwarz, Maureen T. *Fighting Colonialism with Hegemonic Culture: Native American Appropriation of Indian Stereotypes*. Albany: State University of New York Press, 2013.

Shapiro, Nina. "Native Lawyer Takes on Tribes That Kick Members out." *Seattle Times*. December 15, 2015. http://www.seattletimes.com/seattle-news/northwest/native-lawyer-takes-on-tribes-that-kick-members-out/.

Shreve, Braadley. *Red Power Rising: The National Indian Youth Council and the Origins of Native Activism*. Norman: University of Oklahoma Press, 2011.

Simpson, Audra. *Mohawk Interrupts: Political Life Across the Borders of Settler States*. Durham, NC: Duke University Press, 2014.

Simpson, Leanne. "Indict the System: Indigenous and Black Connected Resistance." *Leanne Betasamosake Simpson*, November 28, 2014. http://leannesimpson.ca/indict-the-system-indigenous-black-connected-resistance/.

———. *Islands of Decolonial Love: Stories and Songs*. Winnipeg, Manitoba: ARP Books, 2013.

———. "Not Murdered and Not Missing: Rebelling Against Colonial Gender Violence." In *Taking Sides: Revolutionary Solidarity and the Poverty of Liberalism*, edited by Cindy Milstein, 114–23. Edinburgh, UK and Oakland, CA: AK Press, 2015.

Simpson, Leanne Betasamosake. "The Place Where We All Live and Work Together: A Gendered Analysis of 'Sovereignty.'" In *Native Studies Keywords*, edited by Stephanie Nohelani Teves, Andrea Smith, and Michelle Raheja, 18–24. Tucson: University of Arizona Press, 2015.

Sledd, James. "Bi-Dialectalism: The Linguistics of White Supremacy." *English Journal* 58, no. 9 (December 1969): 1307–15.

Smith, Paul Chaat, and Robert Warrior. *Like A Hurricane: The American Indian Movement from Alcatraz to Wounded Knee*. Boston: South End Press, 1995.

Smitherman, Geneva. " 'A New Way of Talkin': Language, Social Change, and Political Theory." In *Talkin That Talk: Language, Culture, and Education in African America*, 93–108. New York: Routledge, 1999.

———. *Talkin and Testifyin: The Language of Black America*. Detroit: Wayne State University Press, 1986.

———. "The Chain Remain the Same: Communicative Practices in the Hip Hop Nation." *The Black Scholar* 28, no. 1 (1997): 3–25.

———. *Word From the Mother: Language and African Americans*. New York: Routledge, 2006.

Spears, Arthur. "African-American Language Use: Ideology and So-Called Obscenity." In *African-American English: Structure, History and Use*, edited by Salikoko Mufwene, John Rickford, Guy Bailey, and John Baugh, 226–50. London and New York: Routledge, 1998.

Stiglitz, Joseph. *Globalization and Its Discontents*. New York: W. W. Norton & Co., 2002.

Tengan, Ty P. Kawika. *Native Men Remade: Gender and Nation in Contemporary Hawai'i*. Durham, NC: Duke University Press, 2008.

Theriot, Matthew, and Barber Parker. "Native American Youth Gangs: Linking Culture, History and Theory for Improved Understanding, Prevention and Intervention." *Journal of Ethnicity in Criminal Justice* 5, no. 4 (2007): 83–97.

Thrush, Coll. "Hauntings as Histories: Indigenous Ghosts and the Urban Past in Seattle." In *Phantom Past, Indigenous Presence: Native Ghosts in North American Culture and History*, edited by Coll Thrush and Colleen Boyd, 54–81. Lincoln: University of Nebraska Press, 2011.

———. *Native Seattle: Histories from the Crossing-Over Place*. Seattle: Washington University Press, 2007.

Tohoe, Laura. "There Is No Word for Feminism in My Language." *Wicazo Sa Review* 15, no. 2 (Autumn 2000): 103–10.

Troutman, John. *Indian Blues: American Indians and the Politics of Music, 1879–1934*. Norman: University of Oklahoma Press, 2009.

Troutman, John W. "Steelin' the Slide: Hawai'i and the Birth of the Blues Guitar." *Southern Cultures*, Global Southern Music, September 2013, 26–52.

Tuck, Eve, and K. Wayne Yang. "Decolonization Is Not a Metaphor." *Decolonization: Indigeneity, Education and Society* 1, no. 1 (2012): 1–40.

Ullestad, Neal. "American Indian Rap and Reggae: Dancing to the 'Beat of a Different Drummer.'" *Popular Music & Society* 23, no. 2 (1999): 62–90.

Utley, Ebony. *Rap and Religion: Understanding the Gangsta's God*. Santa Barbara, CA: ABC-CLIO, 2012.

Veran, C. "Native Tongues: A Roundtable on Hip Hop's Global Indigenous Movement with Darryl 'DLT' Thompson, Litefoot, Grant Leigh Saunders, Mohammed Yunus Rafiq, and Jaas." In *That's the Joint!: The Hip-Hop Studies Reader*, edited by Mark Anthony Neal and Mark Foreman, Second., 336–44. New York: Routledge, 2012.

Warrior, Robert. *Tribal Secrets: Recovering American Indian Intellectual Traditions*. Minneapolis: University of Minnesota Press, 1995.

Watkins, S. C. *Hip Hop Matters: Politics, Pop Culture, and the Struggle for the Soul of a Movement*. Boston: Beacon Press, 2005.

Weaver, Hilary N. "Urban and Indigenous: The Challenges of Being a Native American in the City." *Journal of Community Practice* 20 (2012): 470–88.

Weaver, Jace. *The Red Atlantic: American Indigenes and the Making of the Modern World, 1000–1927*. Chapel Hill: University of North Carolina Press, 2014.

Williams, Rhonda Y. "'Something's Wrong Down Here': Poor Black Women and Urban Struggles for Democracy." In *African American Urban History Since World War II*, 316–36. Chicago: University of Chicago Press, 2009.

Wolfe, Patrick. "Land, Labor, and Difference: Elementary Structures of Race." *The American Historical Review* 106, no. 3 (June 2001): 866–905.

———. "Settler Colonialism and the Elimination of the Native." *Journal of Genocide Research* 8, no. 4 (December 2006): 387–409.

———. *Traces of History: Elementary Structures of Race*. London and New York: Verso, 2016.

Woodson, Carter G. "The Relations of Negroes and Indians in Massachussets." *The Journal of Negro History* 1, no. 5 (1920): 45–57.

Woolford, Andrew. *This Benevolent Experiment: Indigenous Boarding Schools, Genocide, and Redress in Canada and the United States*. Winnipeg: University of Manitoba Press, 2015.

Yellow Horse Brave Heart, Maria, and Lemyra DeBruyn. "The American Indian Holocaust: Healing Historical Unresolved Grief." *American Indian and Alaska Native Mental Health Research* 8, no. 2 (n.d.): 60–82.

Zemke, Kirsten. "Keeping It Real (Indigenous): Hip Hop in Aotearora as Community, Culture, and Consciousness." In *Cultural Studies in Aotearora New Zealand: Identity, Space, and Place*, edited by Claudia Bell and Steve Mattewman, 205–28. South Melbourne, Victoria: Oxford University Press, 2004.

INDEX